AGE
OF FAITH

TIME LIFE BOOKS ®

LIFE WORLD LIBRARY

LIFE NATURE LIBRARY

TIME READING PROGRAM

THE LIFE HISTORY OF THE UNITED STATES

LIFE SCIENCE LIBRARY

INTERNATIONAL BOOK SOCIETY

GREAT AGES OF MAN

TIME-LIFE LIBRARY OF ART

TIME-LIFE LIBRARY OF AMERICA

FOODS OF THE WORLD

GREAT AGES OF MAN

A History of the World's Cultures

AGE OF FAITH

by

ANNE FREMANTLE

and

The Editors of TIME-LIFE Books

TIME INCORPORATED, NEW YORK

THE AUTHOR: Anne Fremantle, a French-born English journalist who became a United States citizen in 1947, is a longtime student and interpreter of the Middle Ages. Her widely varied writings include *The Age of Belief*, a commentary on medieval philosophers, and translations of Englebert's *Lives of the Saints*, as well as three biographies, three novels and a book of poems. For 14 years a lecturer at Fordham University, she is a frequent contributor to *Commonweal* magazine.

THE CONSULTING EDITOR: Leonard Krieger, formerly Professor of History at Yale, now holds the post of University Professor at the University of Chicago. He is the author of *The German Idea of Freedom* and *Politics of Discretion*.

THE COVER: This stained-glass window in Chartres Cathedral depicts the Virgin with Child. The work, which also appears on page 134, was done in the 12th Century.

TIME-LIFE BOOKS

EDITOR
Maitland A. Edey
EXECUTIVE EDITOR
Jerry Korn
TEXT DIRECTOR   ART DIRECTOR
Martin Mann   Sheldon Cotler
CHIEF OF RESEARCH
Beatrice T. Dobie
PICTURE EDITOR
Robert G. Mason
Assistant Text Directors:
Harold C. Field, Ogden Tanner
Assistant Art Director: Arnold C. Holeywell
Assistant Chief of Research: Martha Turner

PUBLISHER
Rhett Austell
General Manager: Joseph C. Hazen Jr.
Planning Director: John P. Sousa III
Circulation Director: Joan D. Manley
Marketing Director: Carter Smith
Business Manager: John D. McSweeney
Publishing Board: Nicholas Benton,
Louis Bronzo, James Wendell Forbes

GREAT AGES OF MAN

SERIES EDITOR: Russell Bourne
Editorial Staff for *Age of Faith:*
Editor: Harold C. Field
Assistant to the Editor: Peter Meyerson
Text Editor: Diana Hirsh
Assistant Text Editor: Anne Horan
Designer: Norman Snyder
Staff Writer: Gerald Simons
Chief Researcher: Carlotta Kerwin
Picture Research: Jessica Perrin Silvers
Text Research: Nancy C. Newman,
Karen Booth, Doris Kinney, Patricia Skinner,
Lilla Zabriskie, Jane M. Furth

EDITORIAL PRODUCTION
Color Director: Robert L. Young
Copy Staff: Marian Gordon Goldman,
Rosalind Stubenberg, Florence Keith
Picture Department: Dolores A. Littles,
Joan T. Lynch
Art Assistants: Douglas Graham, Anne Landry,
Leonard Wolfe, David Wyland

The following individuals and departments of Time Inc. gave valuable aid in the preparation of this book: the Chief of the LIFE Picture Library, Doris O'Neil; the Chief of the Bureau of Editorial Reference, Peter Draz; the Chief of the TIME-LIFE News Service, Richard M. Clurman; Correspondents Ann Natanson, Erik Amfitheatrof (Rome), Katharine Sachs (London), Elisabeth Kraemer (Bonn), Franz Spelman (Munich), Gertraud Lessing (Vienna), Piero Saporiti (Madrid), Joseph Harriss and Maria Vincenza Aloisi (Paris).

Contents

NOTE: THE ARTISTS AND PRESENT LOCATIONS OF ALL WORKS OF ART REPRODUCED IN THIS BOOK ARE LISTED ON PAGE 187.

Introduction

The thousand medieval years were not solely an "age of faith," nor is faith a uniquely medieval phenomenon. But the cathedrals were the most impressive monuments of that era; its greatest poem was a description of Hell, Purgatory and Paradise; crusades were the only collective enterprises which temporarily rallied all nations; there were heretics and infidels but agnosticism was nonexistent or cowed into silence; the clergy was more numerous and influential in politics, economics, philosophy and other intellectual pursuits than it has ever been since. There is nothing wrong with the traditional formula of an "age of faith," provided we remember that the Middle Ages were many other things as well.

There is something in medieval history for every curiosity. Those of us who are fascinated by the growth of national cultures and their contribution to the composite pattern of Western civilization cannot fail to notice that Europe was born in the Middle Ages. Greco-Roman civilization had its origins on the southernmost European shore of the Mediterranean and spread all around that sea; North Africa and Asia Minor were more essential parts of it than England; Scotland, Scandinavia, Poland were outside the pale. The word of Christ, coming from Palestine, added prestige to the Asiatic provinces of the Roman Empire. At the opening of the Middle Ages, however, the Germans overthrew the Roman barrier which had been cutting Europe in two. Soon a number of missionaries, soldiers and merchants began to fan out toward the outlying regions of the European north and northeast. The Arabs wrested from the Christian world the very lands which had witnessed the first trials and triumphs of its faith, while the pagan lands of outer Europe entered the family of Christian nations.

The home of European civilization was thus located as we know it today—together with the later additions, of course, of America and other "Europes overseas." There is reason to regret that a cleavage between East and West began to appear in the Middle Ages through the sibling rivalry of the Byzantine and Catholic Empires and Churches. But Church and Empire gave the European nations a feeling of unity, while feudalism and town autonomy frustrated all attempts of those bodies to become overbearing monarchies, capable of crushing the infinite variety of national, regional and local manifestations. Ultimately Europe emerged as a mosaic with varied textures, not a flattened surface; as a bundle of private initiatives, not a steamroller in the hands of a despot. That is what made it, and the Middle Ages, great.

Europe, a huge underdeveloped area at the beginning of the Middle Ages, could, by the 13th Century, look with pride on its achievements. This remarkable success was due partly to the legacy of antiquity and to borrowings from the Orient, but above all to the intelligent exertions of Europe's own medieval population. Men are the basic raw material of history. What matters, however, is the way raw material is put to use.

About a thousand years ago, as population began to increase faster and faster, medieval Europe began its remarkable progress. Ingenious men developed better methods of cultivation, better tools and a better distribution of the inhabitants of the land. Commerce among the various sections (which had played second fiddle in antiquity and had sharply declined in the early Middle Ages) became the leading force in economic development. Industry made slower but significant gains. The foundations of modern banking, public finance and accounting were laid.

Economic growth and intellectual achievements proceeded side by side, lending support to each other. The Middle Ages spread literacy among commoners, and trained physicians, lawyers and thinkers in the first universities; medieval traders and preachers ventured all the way to China and tropical Africa. Craftsmen gave glasses to scholars that they might read in old age; alcohol was provided so that they might cheer up. Slavery, which the ancients and even the early churchmen had thought to be inevitable to support the world of free men, almost entirely disappeared. Serfdom also was abolished in some regions and mitigated in others. Free men began toying with representative government and dared to talk back to kings.

Anne Fremantle, long a student of Christian life in the Middle Ages, brings out the main lines of this story with remarkable grace and competence. It is a pleasure to welcome the reader to the medieval pageant as seen by her.

ROBERT S. LOPEZ
Chairman, Medieval Studies, Yale University

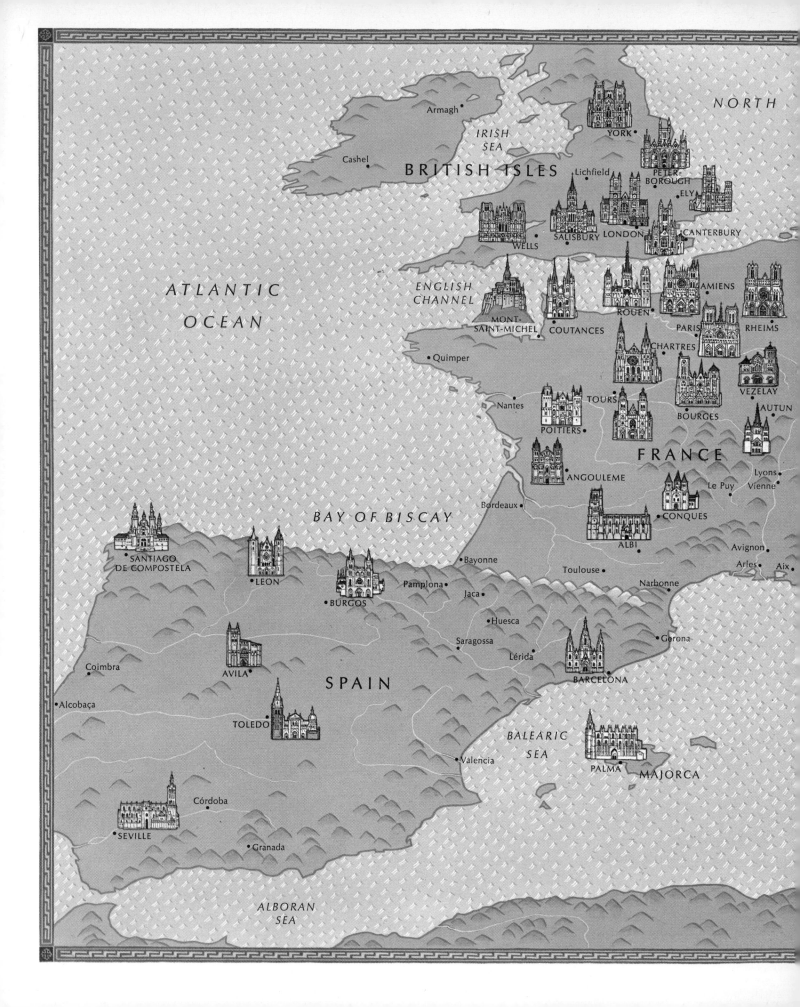

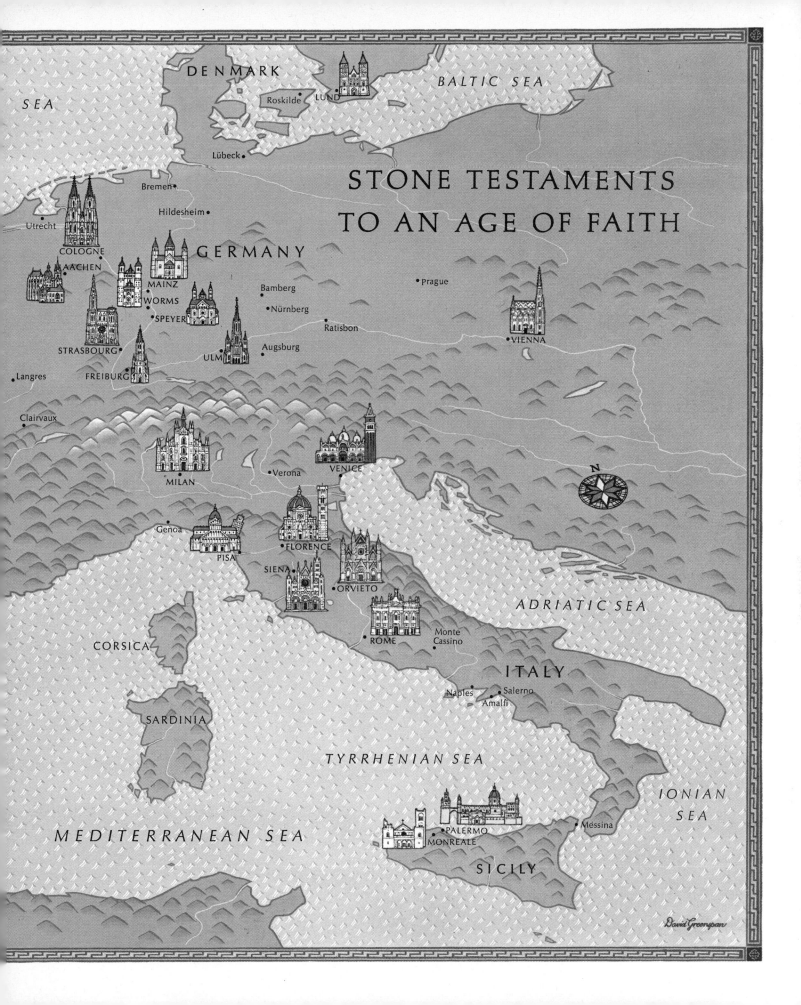

STONE TESTAMENTS
TO AN AGE OF FAITH

SEA

DENMARK

BALTIC SEA

Roskilde • LUND

Lübeck •

Bremen •

Hildesheim •

Utrecht •

COLOGNE

AACHEN

GERMANY

MAINZ

WORMS

SPEYER

Bamberg •

• Prague

• Nürnberg

Ratisbon •

STRASBOURG

ULM

Augsburg •

• VIENNA

Langres •

FREIBURG

Clairvaux •

MILAN

Verona •

VENICE

N

Genoa •

PISA

FLORENCE

SIENA

ORVIETO

ADRIATIC SEA

ROME

Monte
Cassino

CORSICA

ITALY

Naples • • Salerno

SARDINIA

Amalfi •

TYRRHENIAN SEA

*IONIAN
SEA*

MEDITERRANEAN SEA

PALERMO

MONREALE

• Méssina

SICILY

David Greenspan

1

THE RISE OF FEUDALISM

Some 500 years have passed since the close of the chapter of Western history known as the Middle Ages, yet its evidences survive and flourish. The European of today may pay his taxes in the same town halls as his medieval forebears; vote in the same parliament buildings; buy and sell in the same marketplaces; change his money in the same streets; roam the same castles; study within the same college walls; listen to the same bells; and worship in the same cathedrals.

Even to the casual tourist from across the seas, the imprint of the Middle Ages is inescapable. He finds it in the great blue and red windows of Chartres, in the walled battlements of Carcassonne, in the half-timbered houses of Nuremberg, along the Ponte Vecchio in Florence. At Nottingham he may drink an ale at the Trip to Jerusalem, an inn where 12th Century English Crusaders slaked their thirst en route to the Holy Land. At Santiago de Compostela in Spain, he may lodge at a hospice founded by the same Ferdinand and Isabella who financed the journeys of Columbus. At Ypres he may witness a festival, first celebrated about 960, in which cats are flung from the town belfry to symbolize the Belgians' abandonment of pagan gods for Christianity. (In deference to modern sensibilities, stuffed toys now take the place of live animals.)

Beyond the material legacy left us by the Middle Ages, institutions of far more moment in our daily life have come down from that time. Trial by jury, assemblies of elected representatives, middle-class society, universities, banks, the capitalist system itself—all had their roots in an era still often misconstrued as totally bleak and barren, as a thousand years of dark slumber between the grandeur of Rome and the glory of the Renaissance.

The very name, Middle Ages—covering a period from about the second half of the Fifth Century to the first half of the 15th—was a label attached ex post facto by men eager to proclaim their own intellectual advance. This somewhat patronizing designation implied a rekindling of the light of classical times after a prolonged interim in deep shadow. Modern historians reject this view of the medieval era. While much of it was benighted, much of it was spirited and creative. Among the products of its culture were the masters of poly-

CHRIST IN MAJESTY, a major theme for medieval artists, bestows blessings with His right hand while under His left arm He holds a book of the Gospels. This illumination is from a manuscript made for Charlemagne.

phonic music and of cathedral architecture. The works of Dante and Boccaccio, of Giotto and Fra Angelico, heralded the Renaissance.

Along with Dante's lyric genius, it is true, there was wide illiteracy, and below the soaring Gothic spires was the squalor of hovels. For the essence of the Middle Ages lay in its extreme paradoxes. Corruption coexisted with saintliness, ignorance with erudition, bestiality with chivalry, unimaginable devices of torture with exquisite works of artistry.

Beyond these was the greatest paradox of all. Of political unity, medieval Europe actually had little or none. There were successions of kings and dynasties—the Merovingian, the Carolingian, the Capetian, the Ottonian, the Hohenstaufen—but their power was generally short-lived, and their kingdoms uncertain. Of these rulers only the great Carolingian, Charlemagne, wielded his scepter long and well enough to fuse vast areas of the Continent into a cohesive empire. For the most part a central authority was unknown to medieval man. His world was local, sequestered, circumscribed. He was accountable only to his own lord of the manor, understood none but the accents of his own region, and rarely had cause to communicate with his fellow man in another region.

Yet for all their isolation from one another, people of the Middle Ages enjoyed a common bond of surpassing strength: the Christian faith. However physically disjointed, medieval Europe was spiritually a commonwealth—a quasi-real, quasi-ideal entity called Christendom, under the suzerainty of the Pope of Rome. This entity was never static. The forces of another great faith, Islam, continually had to be reckoned with. In time they reft Christendom of most of the eastern Mediterranean lands which it had included at the beginning, and for five centuries they controlled much of Spain, yielding it up to complete Christian re-

conquest only as the Middle Ages drew to an end.

But whatever might be at any given moment its geographical extent, fundamentally medieval Christendom was a unity—the *Respublica Christiana.* This unity was never absolute; it was forever being marred by power struggles between popes and emperors or kings or nobles. Even so, the very fact of its existence pervaded medieval life. All over Europe, there was one Church only. If a man were not baptized into it, he was not a member of society. Anyone excommunicated by the Church lost his political and legal rights as well. At the same time it was the Church which provided sanctuary for those endangered souls who took refuge within its walls. It was the Church which insisted that the poor did not have to fast as much as the rich, and which forbade servile work on Sunday. It was the Church which provided the poor with social services—free food and free hospitalization. There was, for a long while, no other source of education.

The hold the Church had on men's affairs, no less than on their minds, was enormous. Many a king or emperor had a prelate at his side. Charlemagne had his Alcuin, Edgar of England his Dunstan, Charles the Bald of West Frankland his John Scotus Erigena. The occupant of the throne was sometimes as unlettered as his lowliest serf. Charlemagne, though his realm reached from the Elbe to the Adriatic and from the Danube to the Pyrenees, slept with a tablet under his pillow so as to be able to practice the alphabet whenever he woke. Alcuin served him, as other churchmen served their kings, in the capacity of tutor and mentor.

Through its scholarship the Church could also preserve and nurture what was left of the heritage of Roman culture. The Roman pontiffs had remained in the city even after Constantinople had replaced it as the political seat of empire. The

Church and its representatives were thus the sole actual link between the medieval present and the classical past. Among other bequests they transmitted were the Latin language; a respect for the written word; and a corollary zeal for record-keeping based on the Roman concept that *scripta manent*, "what is written endures."

Because from the first Christianity emphasized the value of the individual, in the medieval scheme every person had his place. He had his duties and responsibilities; he also had his rights. All these were scrupulously detailed and recorded in the manorial rolls in England, the accounts of French abbeys, the ledgers and chronicles of Flemish or Italian towns. The survival of such annals has made it possible to know more about the unique way of life of the Middle Ages, in terms of the firsthand, than about any preceding period.

The 10 centuries spanned by the medieval era can be divided, roughly, into halves. The first half was a time of alternating chaos and torpor. The second was a time of growing stability, purposeful institutions and individual awakening. In these later upward-soaring centuries the Roman Empire and the tribes that had overwhelmed it together became Christendom. Once they had settled down, these pagan peoples, with astonishing speed, developed into brisk, busy nations, complete with arts and artifacts. In some cases, Poland and Denmark and Hungary for example, they became admirable examples of forward-looking Christian states within a few decades after the conversion of their leaders. The foundations of the modern world were thus built by former barbarians whose initial entry onto the stage of history had caused terror and upheaval.

They had come, at first, in trickles—Teutonic peoples wandering across the Rhine-Danube frontier to live along Rome's imperial outposts. Then, as their homelands began to suffer the fierce pres-

DANISH MEMORIAL, *a massive stone which King Harald placed over the tomb of his parents at Jelling, has a sculptured Crucifixion (detail above). The oldest representation of Jesus in that country, it was sculptured in the 10th Century, shortly after the Danes' conversion. The figure, in the style of a pagan idol, is a testament to the old religion's survival alongside the new.*

A TYPICAL MANOR *of the 14th Century consisted of the manorhouse (center) and land reserved for the lord's use, his "demesne" (directly behind it), three annually rotated sections of arable land, the village with its church and houses for priest and peasants (right), a common pasture (right foreground), sheep-folds and a mill (left foreground). The priest cultivated a "glebe," or plot, of his own; peasants worked their strips in the fields and small kitchen gardens.*

sures of Hunnish tribes from Asia, they came in hordes, flinging themselves upon the Empire, marauding and looting and burning in their frantic quest for new security. Twice—in 410 and 455—they sacked Rome itself. Just as the world today feels the surge and swell of emerging African nations, so Roman Europe was made aware of assorted strange folk—Visigoths, Ostrogoths, Franks, Alemanni, Burgundians, Jutes, Angles, Saxons, Lombards. Overrunning now this region, now that, these tribes in time vanquished the West—Italy, all Gaul, as far north as Britain, as far south as Spain and North Africa. And even as they settled down in turn, eastern Europe fell to new Asiatic incursions by Avars, Magyars and Bulgars.

In the final analysis the barbarian takeover was one of history's major ironies. The Teutonic tribes had not the slightest intention of destroying Roman culture. The earlier arrivals had been welcomed into the legions of the Caesars and had helped fight off later invaders; some even rose to the rank of general. Occasionally the barbarians evoked rueful admiration. A Fifth Century Christian writer, Salvian, noted: "The Goths lie, but are chaste, the Franks lie, but are generous, the Saxons are savage in cruelty . . . but admirable in chastity. . . . What hope can there be for the Romans when the barbarians are more pure than they?"

The hope, it turned out, was scant. Rome, though beset by internal rot and increasingly too weak to withstand external pressure, had expected as usual to absorb the newcomers. Instead, they prevailed over Rome. The proconsuls and engineers who used to go forth triumphantly to the remotest reaches of the Continent and Britain no longer appeared. The comforts and conveniences they had introduced—hot baths, central heating, main drains, efficient water supplies—fell into disrepair. All over Europe the great light of Roman civilization faded. The times which ensued have sometimes been called the Dark

Ages, a generalization as usual misleading. But assuredly they were parlous times, and they lasted for some 500 years.

During these centuries—the Fifth through the Ninth—Europe relapsed into stagnation. Cities shrank to towns and towns to desolate fields. Paved roads, the pride of the Empire, became rutted, impassable trails. How sharp was the change may be gauged by a comparison of two accounts, one of the Third Century, the other commenting on the Sixth.

The writer of the earlier account was Tertullian, a fervent Christian apologist who, curiously, may have been the originator of the phrase *medium aevum* ("the age in the middle"), which he used in the conviction that his era was merely transitional between classical times and the new day that would come when the Gospel prevailed. Whatever his vision of the future, Tertullian was far from displeased with the present. Surveying the Empire, he wrote: "Delightful farms have now blotted out every trace of the dreadful wastes; cultivated fields have supplanted woods; flocks and herds have driven out wild beasts; sandy spots are sown; rocks and stones have been cleared away; bogs have been drained. Large towns now occupy land hardly tenanted before by cottages. Thick population meets the eye on all sides. We overcrowd the world."

By the Sixth Century, however, Italy had become so dismal that memories of its misery were still vivid 200 years later, when Paul the Deacon recalled: "You saw villas or fortified places filled with people in utter silence. The whole world seemed brought to its ancient stillness: no voice in the field, no whistling of shepherds. The harvests were untouched. Human habitations became the abode of wild beasts."

The stillness of which Paul wrote was a stillness not just of stagnation but of fear. Hunger and disease stalked early medieval man. Ravage by enemies near and far was a constant threat, and too often a

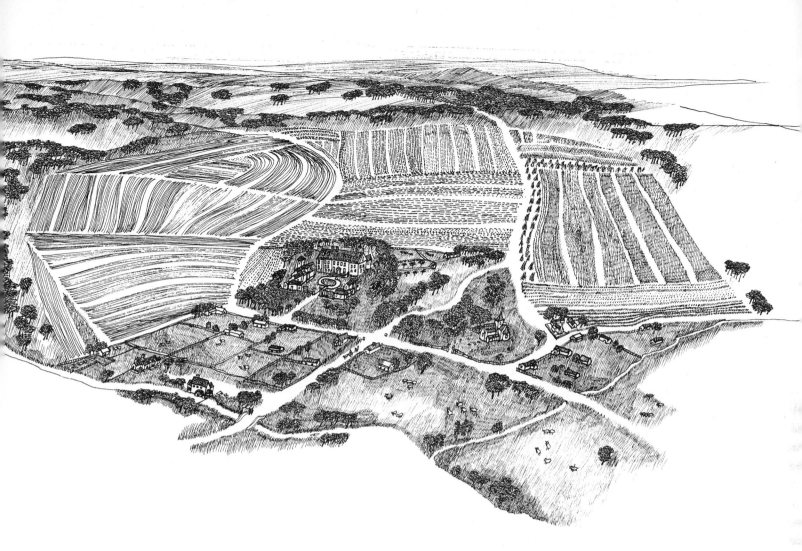

reality. Law and order, the twin pillars of the Roman imperial system, lay in ruins. An individual's sole hope of protection rested in local chieftains powerful enough to fend off a foe. This fact of life began to be reflected in the European landscape. Characteristically, the early medieval community was a huddle of cottages within reassuring reach of the lord's manor house, set in open country and accessible from the next village only by narrow track or path.

Men paid a stiff price for what security they had. In days gone by, many a farmer had worked his own small Apulian field or terraced Provençal vineyard. But this sturdy breed of freeholder had largely vanished. In return for a lord's protection, many peasants became serfs, bound to the lord for life. The distinctions between serfs varied, depending upon the amount of land they were permitted to hold. At the bottom of the ladder were the cotters —from the old Norse *kot*, cottage—who were given

perhaps three or four acres to farm but also had to serve as menials of the manor household. The mass of serfs, called villeins—from *villa*, farm—were given the use of as many as 40 acres and such extras as the right to draw water from the lord's springs and gather wood from his forests. In exchange they had to labor for a prescribed number of days a week on the lord's lands, and to supply him with produce from their own.

An economy wholly dependent upon agriculture is, in the best of times, precarious; in the early Middle Ages it was touch and go. Vast areas of the Continent were still wilderness; even vaster areas were sodden, under water for much of the long northern winter. Available farmland was undercultivated and overcrowded. Famine was endemic, and no respecter of status. Entire royal courts—king, queen, clergy, courtiers—were constantly on the move from one manor of the realm to another as provisions in the first place gave out. Often the local noble was reduced to eating what game he could hunt down in his own preserves—a major reason why manorial justice dealt so harshly with peasant poachers. Inevitably the burdens of this straitened society fell on its workhorse, the serf.

The load was heavy and the exactions strict. From every serf on the manor two kinds of labor were required: field work and handwork—ditchdigging, tree-cutting, road-mending, manure-carting, chores now associated with the term "handyman." The average manor had from 900 to 3,000 acres to be farmed, and perhaps two dozen families to supply the muscle. The serf was obliged to plow, seed and harvest these acres, and, in addition, perform "boon" work, extra service to signal his gratitude for the lord's protection.

Aelfric the Grammarian, a Saxon writer, gave a glimpse of the serf's life in his *Colloquium:* "Well, ploughman, how do you work?" "Oh, Sir, I work very hard. I go out in the dawning, driving the oxen to the field and I yoke them to the plough. Be the winter never so stark, I dare not stay at home for fear of my lord; but every day I must plough a full acre or more, having yoked the oxen and fastened the share and coulter to the plough." "Have you any mate?" "I have a boy, who drives the oxen with a goad. He is now hoarse from cold and shouting." "Well, is it very hard work?" "Yes, indeed, it is very hard work."

Sweat and strain were the serf's lot, and so were taxes in a variety of guises. The lord could impose a head tax, an income tax, and extra payments in produce for the use of his oven, mill and wine press. Sometimes the serf had to pay for the right to marry a wench from another manor. He could also expect that when he died the lord might strip his cottage of its meager contents.

Escape from this thralldom was possible, but only spasmodically. A late medieval proverb had it that "town air makes free." A serf who could make his way to a town and remain there for a year and a day, paying the town's taxes, was thereby liberated. Sometimes freedom could be bought directly from the lord, for nobles were chronically out of pocket. A serf ambitious enough to put in added time on his own land on feast days might eventually gain his independence with proceeds from the sale of surplus eggs and honey, pigs and chickens he managed to amass beyond the lord's quota.

More often, however, holidays afforded an all too precious breather for the serf. They were a time for horseplay, a time to sing lewd love songs, to frolic about a flower-bedecked maypole, to watch a traveling show with its mumming and masques and dancing bears. These interludes were brief; yet few men of low degree aspired to more. "God hath shapen lives three; boor and knight and priest they be," went the medieval rhyme. If it was so ordained, so be it. The function of the peasantry was to serve the clergy and the nobles, and few questioned its rightness.

But if it was the duty of the peasant to support the ruling classes, they in turn had duties toward him and each other. The churchman had to minister to man's spiritual needs; the noble had to govern and to provide security. Within the aristocracy itself, there existed a complex reciprocity of rights and debts; the idea of *noblesse oblige*, "rank has its obligations," had deep meaning in those days. The relationship of noble and serf, based on the manor, was called manorialism; that of noble and noble was called feudalism, based on the *feudum*, or fief— a grant of land by a superior to a lesser lord, or vassal, in return for his homage and services.

An assortment of causes contributed to the rise of feudalism. As earlier clans broke up and blood ties slackened, geographic proximity became more important; a man rallied to that man whose land marched with his, and together they more easily withstood threats of incursion. In the absence of an economy based on money payments, Europe lived principally by barter, and the exchange of services logically followed.

The feudal relationship forged a contract between two individuals, each responsible and accountable for his actions, protected by the sanctity of the given word. The bond was sealed in a formal act of homage in which the vassal placed his hands between those of his lord and was kissed on the mouth in return. The lord not only proffered the fief and the assurance of its defense against an enemy, but also provided a forum for the settlement of feudal disputes. For his part the vassal took an oath of fealty, pledging himself to be the lord's man, faithfully and for life. There was nothing abject about this arrangement, for in the hierarchal scheme of medieval nobility, with its knights and barons, counts and dukes, kings and emperors, a vassal might have his own vassals, a lord his own overlords. One of the greatest of the later medieval aristocrats, the Count of Champagne, numbered many nobles as his vassals, and himself owed homage to the Abbot of Saint-Denis, the Archbishop of Rheims, the Duke of Burgundy, the King of France and the Emperor of Germany.

The services rendered by a vassal to his lord included some that were civil, some financial and some military. He had to attend the lord's court and help him mete out justice, sitting as associate judge in the trial of another vassal, who had the right to this treatment by his peers. He was obliged to pay the lord a fee when he took over his fief. (In late medieval times, he had to pay another fee if part of his land changed hands.) He had to provide lodging if the lord and his retinue happened to be passing through. Above all, he owed military service to his lord, both castle guard and combat duty. When summoned by his lord, he had to appear in the field with a fighting troop made up of his own vassals, on horseback and in armor, the

FEUDAL RELATIONSHIPS *are recalled by a 12th Century seal (above) and a 13th Century bronze vessel. The seal shows a vassal kneeling before his lord in the act of homage. Their clasped hands indicate that the vassal has volunteered his allegiance to the lord. The vessel, kept in the church, served as a receptacle for tithes paid by the peasants in the form of grain. This vessel, from France, has legs shaped like dragons' snouts and is encircled with three decorative bands: at top peasants are dancing; at center is a hunt with falcons; bottom is a flowered scroll pattern.*

number being roughly calculated on the size and resources of his fief; each of his vassals in turn supplied his own soldiers. The mounted man's fighting service was at the core of the feudal system; the knight—in French, *chevalier*, man-on-horseback—provided the system's sinews.

The structure of the feudal system gradually emerged in the wake of a great seven-day battle at Poitiers, in southern France, in October 732, between the recently Christianized Franks and invading Arab Moslems. Most of the Franks were on foot, all of the Arabs on horse. The Franks stood solid—"as a wall," one observer put it—and won. But the Arabs' superior mobility, and their use of a strange new device, stirrups, which enabled them to fight from horseback, offered a lesson which the ruler of the Franks, Charles Martel, learned quickly and well. He ordered that henceforth his men, as a price for his protection, would have to provide themselves with horse, stirrups, armor, and whatever supplies were required; thus equipped, they would have to fight in their protector's service. To be able to afford these expenses, knights needed income. Martel took care of this by seizing Church lands and parceling them out to his warriors. Martel's order was fine in theory but observance was so spotty that it was a failure in practice.

Even as it hastened the arrival of feudalism and helped change the basis of Western warfare from infantry to cavalry units, Poitiers served as a turning point in another way as well. For never again would the fearsome armies of Islam advance so deeply into Europe. For a long time thereafter, striking out from their African empire, they would continue to bedevil the southern fringes of the European continent; they achieved and retained a firm hold on Spain, southern Italy and the Mediterranean islands. But the heartland of Europe was henceforth free of this menace.

Other menaces, from other directions, persisted.

THE EMPEROR CHARLEMAGNE, *carrying an orb to symbolize worldly power, was the first Christian monarch to be sculpted in an equestrian statue. Cast in the Ninth Century, this bronze is believed to be modeled after one of Roman Emperor Marcus Aurelius.*

Poitiers did not suddenly put a halt to all the convulsive arrivals and departures of peoples and races which marked these confused early centuries of the Middle Ages. Nevertheless, it reflected a ray of hope, a promise of stability to come. The hope and the promise were destined to be realized, for five bright decades, by Charles Martel's grandson, Charlemagne. In any age Charlemagne would have been memorable; in his own times, he was unique.

He was big and blond, more than six foot four, with a long nose, lively eyes and a high-pitched voice. His neck was too short and his "belly too prominent," according to the candid memoir of his secretary, Eginhard, but these flaws were masked by his generally fine proportions and his grace of movement. He strode about, sword always girt, in silver-bordered tunic, gartered hose, a doublet of otter and sable skins, and a blue cloak. He exercised a good deal and, like his hard-living gentry, loved to ride and hunt and roister. He enjoyed pomp and ceremony, and the company of women; he had five wives and numerous mistresses.

If Charlemagne was a man of large appetites, he was also a man of large vision and enterprise. His vision was no more, no less than to restore the power and glory of imperial Rome. He succeeded brilliantly. From the time he became King of the Franks in 768 to his death in 814, all of western Europe except England, Scandinavia, southern Italy and Moslem Spain had fallen to him. On Christmas Day in 800, Charlemagne's triumph was consecrated by his coronation in St. Peter's as the new head of the Roman Empire in the West.

Few events were to leave a deeper mark on the history of Europe. Although under Charlemagne's weakling heirs the Empire was fated to fall apart, some 150 years after his death it was to be revived by a great German King, Otto I, as the Holy Roman Empire, minus France this time, but incorporating Germany and northern Italy. It would flourish as a great reality until the 13th Century and linger as a reality of sorts until the 19th. It would be mocked by Voltaire as neither holy nor Roman nor empire, its borders would be reduced, yet to its declining days it would continue to cast its shadow on the map, the politics and the shifting strategies of Europe.

Charlemagne's acquisition of the title and crown of Emperor had another equally vital and more immediate outcome. It launched an era of recurrent tension and open conflict between Church and state. This epic struggle—essentially a battle between the papacy and the Empire for supremacy one over the other—went on for six centuries, but a hint of its intricacies appeared in the very circumstances of Charlemagne's coronation. As his indefatigable chronicler, Eginhard, recalled it, Charlemagne had gone to St. Peter's for no other reason than the observance of the Christmas service. As he arose from prayer, Pope Leo III placed a crown upon his head and, to the applause of throngs of onlookers, acclaimed him as Carolus Augustus. Charlemagne, who had thought to make himself Emperor, and at a time and under conditions of his own choosing, was annoyed—and outmaneuvered. Had he known in advance, Eginhard asserted, the monarch "would not have entered the church, great festival though it was."

Charlemagne's bequest to later generations was a monumental one. Whatever it left in the way of political and religious difficulties to be resolved, it also left a firm foundation on which a higher civilization could be built. Charlemagne genuinely loved learning; the schools which he founded, under the direction of his beloved counselor Alcuin, fostered the spread of literacy and scholarship, thus ultimately leading to the establishment of universities. He was an active patron of the arts. The Carolingian Renaissance, named for him, foreshadowed the great surge of esthetic achievement memorialized in

Romanesque and Gothic architecture and sculpture.

His wide-ranging curiosity extended to the most prosaic details of life. He is thought to have encouraged the three-field system of agriculture which, together with the introduction of the heavy plow and the digging of dikes and canals for drainage, spurred food production all over Europe. Under this new method of farming, arable land was divided roughly into three parts: one sown in the fall with winter wheat or rye, or with barley or oats; one sown the following spring with legumes —peas, chick-peas, lentils or beans; and one part left fallow. The next year the first part was spring-sown, the third fall-sown, and the second left fallow, permitting the legumes to fix the nitrogen in the soil. Peas and beans were a staple of the medieval diet, rich or poor; as the English rhyme put it, "Pease porridge hot, pease porridge cold, pease porridge in the pot, nine days old."

Charlemagne's long reign in effect wrote finis to the darker side of medieval history, although, as always in the march of civilization, the arrival of a better day was slow and protracted. Throughout the Ninth Century, after the Emperor's death, Europe had to contend with a second barbarian onslaught, this time primarily from the Viking North. Against the fierce Norsemen new and stronger defenses had to be devised. Gradually Europe began to take on the look still today associated with the word "medieval."

Towns and monasteries sprouted thick new walls; fortified castles began to be built. Later, in the 12th Century, these would become massive stone creations with towers, drawbridges and portcullis gates. But until stone could be quarried in large amounts, the early castles were more like the log forts of the American frontier: square, timbered blockhouses, strategically located upon a hill, or at the edge of a cliff, or in the loop of a river. As peasants began to cluster in their protective shadows, the castles became the focus of life in evolving medieval villages.

Within the castle keep—its innermost stronghold —a typical daily scene would be one of incredible noise and activity. Smiths would be sharpening and burnishing swords or shoeing horses. Archers would be practicing. Grooms would be exercising horses, and purging or poulticing the sick; others would be feeding the livestock. Carpenters would be making or mending the trestle tables and long benches that were, except for the big beds, the castle's only furniture. There would be an incessant din—of hounds, horses, falcons, cattle, men.

Somewhere, too, there would be the sound of someone being hurt, for, contrary to the romantic illusion, castle life could be distinctly nasty and brutish. Every castle, however small, had its dungeon. Punishments were primitive, coarse and cruel. Men were beaten, branded, mutilated, their eyes gouged out or their hands cut off. Torture was habitual; it only grew more refined as time went on. Justice was done by trial by hot iron or cold water. Thrown into water, the accused was guilty if he floated. A shrewd man would expel his breath, sink and hope for rescue before it was too late. And work-hardened hands, armored with horny calluses, could grasp a hot iron bar and show no signs of festering after three days, sure proof of innocence. Or, if two claimants appeared in a case, "judicial combat" might be their fate. They had to fight with wooden shields and sharp picks until one yielded; he then was adjudged guilty and, often, hanged forthwith.

For anyone with any interest in a life beyond the manifestations of physical force, there was a way out: the cloister. As more and more men elected to take this road, their individual decisions had a momentous collective impact. The Church to which they dedicated themselves was the greatest spiritual power in medieval Europe. Now it was to become a great temporal power as well.

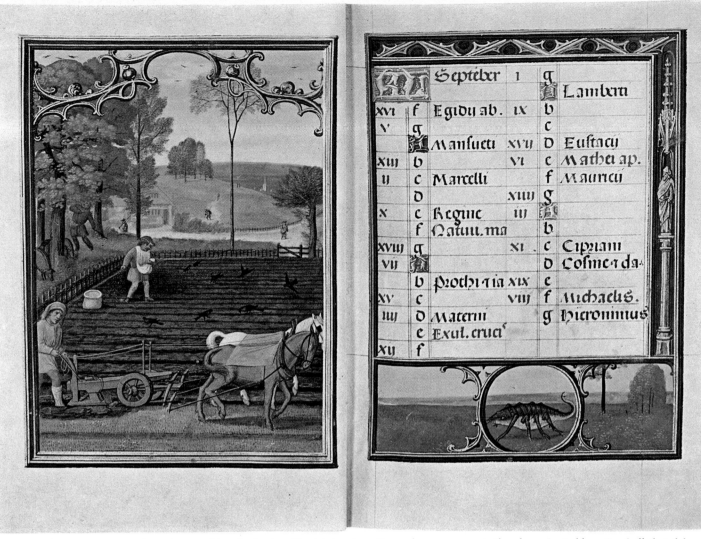

A SEPTEMBER PLOWING SCENE *faces the month's calendar in a Flemish breviary. To work-worn peasants the plow was emblematic of all their labors.*

THE PEASANT'S CALENDAR OF TOIL

Only about 10 per cent of medieval people lived in towns; most of the rest were peasants on manorial farms. The average peasant had a small holding of land, a rude home with thatched roof and dirt floor, and heavy obligations to render work and produce to his lord. His whole world—his village, the manorhouse, the surrounding fields and woods—might encompass less than two square miles.

The peasant's life, illustrated on these pages with scenes from a Flemish prayer book, was governed (as always with farmers) by the seasons. Each autumn, the peasants sowed wheat and rye; each spring they planted other grains plus legumes; each summer they harvested both crops. Between these periods of backbreaking labor came many lesser chores, with only brief respites. The peasants' toil brought them uncertain returns, and it shortened their lifetime to a brief span—even less than that of the violent lords, who often risked death in battle.

When April with his showers sweet

The drought of March hath pierced to the root...

Zephyr with his sweet breath

quickens the tender shoots...

And small birds make melody....

—GEOFFREY CHAUCER

Mavus —*May*

Spring on the manor began as soon as seasonal rains had softened the earth enough for plowing. The peasants sowed their plots—and the lord's—with the crops celebrated in an old folk song: "Oats, peas, beans and barley grow." In addition, each family had its own garden to plant with leeks, beets, cabbage, and its own livestock to put out to pasture. In April, with the cows in milk again *(opposite)*, the peasant's wife was kept busy making butter and cheese—and saving up the payment of eggs due to the lord at Easter.

Spring planting was finished by Holy Week, and after that the peasants' life was relatively easy for a few weeks. They thronged into church for the impressive ceremonies of Eastertide, and not long afterward they celebrated another festival that bespoke their pagan heritage—May Day, with its abandoned dancing and singing. But May also brought many chores. The peasants repaired house and barn, fixed fences, hedgerows and drainage ditches. To protect their flocks from a new generation of predators, peasant bands hiked to the woods to "seek out and capture the wolf-cubs with poison, staves, pits and dogs." On their way to and fro, or while hoeing the manorhouse garden, the men often glimpsed the elegant life their labors supported: the lord's guests boating *(left)* or riding out on the hunt *(background)*.

When men beginneth to weed

The thistle from the seed

In summer...

God give them good speed,

And long good life to lead.

—ANONYMOUS, ENGLAND

For peasants everywhere, the work load grew heavier as the days grew warmer. Early in June vinedressers in France and Germany had to tend their vines. English and Flemish herdsmen washed their sheep, and shearers (*opposite, top*) clipped off the wool under the eye of the lord's steward (with staff). By now the fields needed weeding, but many peasants put off the job in the belief that thistles cut before June 24 would grow back threefold.

That date, Midsummer Day, ushered in the year's busiest months. "In certain regions," one observer wrote, "the boys collect bones and certain other rubbish, and burn them, and. . . . go about the fields with the brands"—to drive away dragons. The next morning, the hay harvest began; in the Flemish scene shown at bottom on the opposite page, grain is delivered for grinding at the windmill in the distance while the hay-mowing proceeds in the foreground. Women and children worked side by side with the men, and they brought in the lord's share before their own. If the hay was gathered by August 1, it was none too soon, for now the two major crops, rye and wheat, were ripe for harvest. The peasants labored on through August, fighting exhaustion as well as heat. It was not until late September that they sat down to the long-awaited harvest-home supper.

Auguſtus *—August*

Iunius —June

Iulius —July 25

I have but one story—The stags are moaning, The sky is snowing, Summer is gone.

—ANONYMOUS, IRELAND

ꟽouanb —*November*

Autumn was the season for storing away supplies and foodstuffs for the winter. The peasants brought in vegetables from their own small gardens, picked fruit in the orchards, exercised their customary rights in the manor's forest by gathering firewood and shaking down acorns and beechnuts to feed their hogs.

Each harvested crop required processing. The wheat was threshed with wooden flails and flung into the air to winnow the grain from the straw and the chaff. In October, in France, the grapes were trampled in vats and the fermented wine was put in casks. In November Flemish peasants beat the dried stalks of flax with heavy "scutchers" *(left)* to separate the woody pith from the valuable fiber that would be spun into thread. "Blood-month," the time for slaughtering livestock, came in October in some countries, in November in others.

With fodder always in short supply, the peasants drove to market all the cattle they could not feed through the winter. The Flemish scene opposite shows a bull changing hands outside a slaughterhouse, while in the background a townsman on a ladder picks fruit from his lone tree. The price of a bull or cow was always an important sum. In terms of food, one animal, preserved in salt and rationed out prudently in stews, could provide a peasant family with meat through the winter.

The bitter frosts, with the sleet and rain,

Destroyed hath the green in every field...

—GEOFFREY CHAUCER

December —December

The 12 days of Christmas brought to a climax the peasants' long holiday season of feasting, churchgoing and folk festivities. The big meal on Christmas Day was traditionally served up by the lord, and all the peasants were invited. For their main course a pig might be killed *(above)* and its blood used in a pudding. Often the men were permitted "to sit drinking after dinner in the manor hall."

After the holidays, harsh weather cur- tailed the men's activities, but not their wives'. The women cooked, wove cloth and made clothes; and some were called to wait upon the lord or his functionaries, who were content to warm themselves by the fire *(right)*. Through January little work could be done out of doors. But in Febru- ary—descriptively called "Mud-month" by Charlemagne—the peasant began spread- ing the fields with manure and sharpening his plow for the labors of another spring.

Ianuarius —January

2

THE LIGHT OF THE CHURCH

In the pall that spread over Europe during the early Middle Ages, one light alone continued to shine: that of the Church. Many of its clergy were killed, its property was despoiled, yet it survived and grew stronger. One by one the pagan peoples who had wrecked the old order embraced the Church. From it they took not only spiritual but temporal guidance, for within its ranks dwelt the only men qualified to build a civilization anew.

That the Church could fulfill this role was a testament both to its innate vitality and its superb gift for organization. When the barbarian irruption began, Christianity was only four centuries old, and for more than half that time it had been an imperiled and persecuted sect. Still it had managed to arrange its own house, and to structure it against stress and strain. In the centuries to come, the Church would develop a clearly defined system of government and hierarchy of officers. The basic unit of organization, the diocese, was presided over by a bishop, whose headquarters were in a town; assisting him, and tending to the sick and poor, were deacons; in rural communities within the diocese, Church affairs were managed by a priest, who took his name from the *presbyter*, or elder, of Scripture.

After Christianity was made the official religion of the Roman Empire in 380, the structure of the Church became more elaborate. The bishops in the chief towns of the imperial provinces came to be known as archbishops, those in the premier cities of the Empire—Rome, Constantinople, Antioch, Jerusalem, Alexandria—as patriarchs. The Roman patriarch was pre-eminent; he could claim direct succession from the first Bishop of Rome, the Apostle Peter, to whom, according to the Gospel, Christ had said: "Thou art Peter, and upon this rock I will build my Church; and the gates of hell shall not prevail against it. And I will give unto thee the keys of the kingdom of heaven: and whatsoever thou shalt bind on earth shall be bound in heaven: and whatsoever thou shalt loose on earth shall be loosed in heaven."

While willing to accord the Roman patriarch especial respect, his fellow patriarchs were less ready to accord him supremacy. After the shift of imperial power to Constantinople—essentially a withdrawal to a defensible position against the rising tide of barbarism in the West—the Eastern churchmen argued that the patriarch of that city merited an ecclesiastical authority co-equal with that of the Roman. But a declaration to this effect, at a council at Chalcedon in Asia Minor in 451, met with a rejoinder by the Roman patriarch, Leo the Great, asserting the primacy of his office.

Leo did not have the exclusive title of Pope; as yet this name—in Latin, *papa*, father—was also applied to other bishops and even to priests, and not for several centuries was its use reserved for the Roman pontiff. Nevertheless it was through Leo that the theory of papal supremacy became explicit. His emphatic enunciation of the Petrine succession—the unbroken line of the bishops of Rome from St. Peter to himself—provided a basis for later assertions of absolute papal infallibility in the areas of faith and morals. The pronouncements of Chalcedon were fateful on another score. Increasingly thereafter, the gap widened between the eastern, Greek-speaking sector of the Church and the western, Latin-speaking sector, even as between the eastern and western halves of the Empire itself.

Christianity's emergence as a state religion had consequences for the Church externally no less than internally. While still an oppressed minority, Christians had come to regard their faith as *catholica*, universal; many argued that those who were outside the Christian community could not attain salvation. Official recognition of the Church afforded effective opportunity to discourage those who quarreled with any part of Catholic doctrine. By imperial fiat they were labeled heretics. Their meetings were broken up, books which contained their teachings were burned, and their property was confiscated. With increasing frequency, those who refused to renounce their heresies were put to death.

Imperial edicts augmented the power of the Church in other ways. Its lands and clergy were exempt from taxes. Church officials charged with minor crimes were allowed to be tried in Church rather than civil courts. One of the most far-reaching decrees permitted the Church to receive bequests of money and property. This ruling, coupled with the practice adopted by the emperor of building great basilicas as places of worship suitable for a state faith, launched a tradition that long outlived the Empire. Henceforth kings and nobles throughout Europe would deem it a mark of virtue to endow the Church with some of their worldly wealth. The churches and monasteries grew ever more affluent; in later centuries, their income from landholdings alone would exceed the revenues of any one country of Europe.

By the time of the barbarian onslaught of the Fifth Century, the Church was sufficiently entrenched to weather the storm, and nowhere more notably than in its stronghold at Rome. The Roman bishops had filled the power vacuum created when the imperial apparatus was moved east. They had taken over control of such temporal matters as the election of city officials and the spending of public funds. The habit of leadership persisted even in the face of invasion. It was Leo the Great who personally went forth to confront Attila, the dread Hun, outside of Rome and persuaded him to spare the city.

Throughout Europe, wherever the turmoil subsided and barbarian rule took root, the new masters came to rely more and more upon the civilizing counsel of men of the Church. As experienced administrators, and as custodians of the knowledge and learning of the past, these men started Europe on its slow, upward climb out of chaos. Foremost among them, fittingly, were the monks—those disciplined individuals who had felt strongly enough about the chaos, and the concurrent decline in the

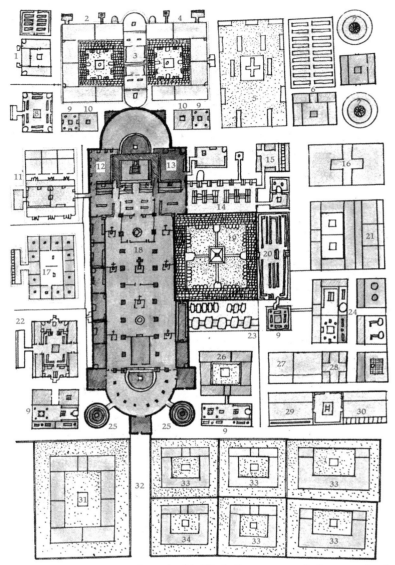

THE IDEAL MONASTERY, *as shown in this Ninth Century ground plan, was a hard-working community with the church as its center. Since this plan was a general guide, not a blueprint, not all monasteries had all the elements listed below.*

1. Doctor
2. Hospital
3. Chapel
4. Novitiate
5. Cemetery
6. Gardener
7. Poultry
8. Leeching house
9. Kitchens
10. Baths
11. Abbot's house
12. Scriptorium and library
13. Vestry
14. Monks' sitting room and dormitory
15. Latrine
16. Barn
17. School
18. Abbey church
19. Cloister
20. Refectory
21. Craftsmen's workshops
22. Guesthouse
23. Storage cellar
24. Bakery, brewery, mill, wine press
25. Towers
26. Almonry
27. Coopery
28. Granary
29. Horses
30. Cattle
31. Hostel (probably)
32. Entrance
33. Livestock
34. Servants

old virtues and verities, to do something about it, first in their own private lives and then in the world around them.

The ascetic way of life they chose and practiced —monasticism—antedated Christianity in its origins. In the East, centuries before Christ, the followers of Buddha had chosen to leave the world while continuing to live in it. Christ had shown His disciples the desert, and early in the Christian era anchorites, or hermits—at first singly, then in small groups—followed Him there. Eremitic monasticism, however, never gained substantial hold in Europe. Instead Europeans preferred the organized monastic life—communal, or cenobitic, monasticism.

One individual, above all others, molded the form of Western monasticism: an Italian patrician named Benedict of Nursia. Born near Spoleto about 480, he was sent to Rome to be educated. Although merely 12 at the time—still stripling enough to be accompanied by his nurse—he soon took the measure of the city's decadence and depravity. At 20 he abandoned this milieu for a lonely cave high on a cliff in wild country south of Rome. In an earlier time the area had been a favorite of that most profligate of tyrants, the Emperor Nero; a palace he had built there was now given over to underbrush. Benedict stayed for three years in his eyrie overlooking this erstwhile scene of robust pleasures. He wore a hair shirt, the rough and scratchy garment traditionally worn by those who wish to mortify the flesh. His diet was bread, which a faithful friend lowered to him every day from above the cliff in a basket on a rope.

After a time Benedict reassessed the value of solitude and self-torment. In later years, to an extremist who had chained himself in a cave, he sent a message noting that "the true servant of God is chained not to rocks by iron, but to righteousness by Christ." In place of solo displays of extravagant piety Benedict came to feel that a more constructive end would be served by group living and hard work. In 529, on the heights of Monte Cassino north of Naples, he founded a monastery to put his idea into effect. Monte Cassino was destined for more than its share of vicissitudes, lasting into our own era. Five times it was destroyed, and five times rebuilt. The first to demolish it were Lombards on foot in 580; the last were Allied bombers in 1944, seeking to root out Nazi troops believed to be dug in there. (When its abbey was restored after World War II, the paneled bronze doors depicted the barbarians and the flyers in adjacent bas-reliefs.)

To guide life at his monastery, Benedict drew up a comprehensive set of regulations. The monastery was to be self-sustaining and self-governing. Poverty and chastity were to mark its way of life. Its head, the abbot, was to be elected by the monks. Each man who wished to become a monk had to take vows of obedience, of "conversion of life" (a promise to improve himself spiritually), and of stability, binding himself to the monastic community for life. His day was divided into one part prayer, one part sleep, and one part intellectual and manual labor—reading, teaching, domestic chores, farming. He was explicitly forbidden to risk his health by inordinate fasting. The Benedictine way was moderate and merciful.

The Rule of St. Benedict—as his regulations became collectively known—worked so well that it has served ever since as the model for all Western monastic communities. Living by the rule—in Latin, *regula*—monks came in time to be called regular clergy, as distinct from the secular clergy, those who lived in the *saeculum*, the world.

The latter half of the Middle Ages would see a vast expansion of the monastic movement, and the establishment of new orders of monks, each with its special character. The Cluniacs would do battle against growing Church corruption and laxity. The Camaldolese, Carthusians and Cistercians would in varying degrees revive the early Christian mode of austere living in remote fastnesses. The Franciscans—founded by the gentle Francis of Assisi—and the Dominicans would become mendicant friars, and go among the people preaching rather than shut themselves up in cloisters. But until the first of these new orders, the Cluniacs, appeared in the 10th Century, the Benedictines provided the main thrust of monasticism.

From the starting point of Monte Cassino, hundreds of Benedictine communities sprang up. Their influence upon a Europe shattered and spent was incalculable. The grain fields, gardens, orchards and fishponds of the monasteries became the proving grounds of new agricultural techniques. Their libraries were the repositories of manuscripts which had escaped the havoc of repeated barbarian invasions. In their *scriptoria* monks copied and thereby perpetuated the works of Vergil, Ovid, Caesar and Cicero, and the Latin translations of the Greeks. Monks also wove their own cloth, made their own wine and were their own carpenters and masons. They transmitted these useful arts to the people of the surrounding countryside. The sick and the starving were attended in monastery hospitals; those wanting to learn were taught in monastery schools; those traveling far from home were lodged in monastery guesthouses.

Many who glimpsed in passing the serenity and relative security of the cloistered life found its appeal irresistible. Among those who joined the communities were social outcasts seeking haven, idlers who envisioned a soft berth, and men who had no stomach for soldiering or for the raw brutality of the outside world. But there were also those who wished to study and write in quietude, and, as from the beginning of Christianity, those motivated solely by a desire for the delights of contemplation.

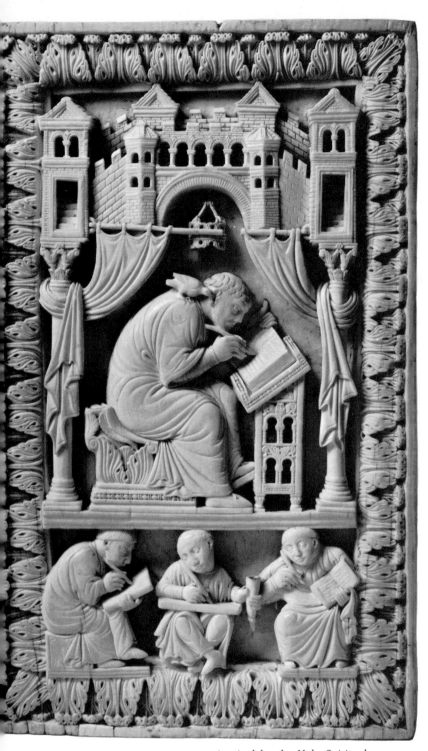

GREGORY THE GREAT, *inspired by the Holy Spirit—shown as a dove—writes as scribes copy his manuscript. Although separated for artistic reasons in this 10th Century ivory panel, the author and his scribes worked together in one room—the scriptorium.*

The Benedictine discipline so shaped its adherents that from their numbers, over the ages, the Church drew several thousand of its bishops and archbishops and 24 of its popes. The first monk to become Pope, in 590, was Gregory the Great, one of St. Benedict's early followers, and like him born of a noble and wealthy Italian family.

As Pope, Gregory never lost sight of one of the most cherished of Benedictine aims: conversion of the heathen. Legend had it that he harbored the memory of some fair-haired lads from Britain whom he had observed being auctioned off in the Roman slave market; had they the faith, he is said to have remarked, they would be "not Angles, but Angels." He had sought in vain to be allowed to undertake a personal mission to Britain. Now, exercising his papal prerogative, he launched a missionary enterprise that would fundamentally transform the Church and the world.

Like a chain reaction, missionizing in one region produced those who would carry the Gospel elsewhere. The first to go forth, in 596, were a Benedictine prior of Rome, Augustine, and 40 of his monks, bearing a silver cross and a picture of Christ. Southern England was their target and triumph; Augustine became the first Archbishop of Canterbury. As the English Church flourished, it, in turn, sent its sons to the Continent. The most effective was an Eighth Century Devonshire-born monk, Winfrith, whom the Pope later renamed Boniface, "doer of good." St. Boniface virtually singlehandedly organized and disciplined the German Church. By the 10th Century, almost all the Continent would be Christian.

In the wake of the missionaries came the organizers. Churches were built, the diocesan system established and monasteries founded—all approved by the newly converted rulers. In theory, these men recognized the spiritual primacy of the Church, but few actually accepted the radical conversion from pagan morality that their new faith demanded of them. Despite mass baptisms in which they led as many as 10,000 of their followers into the Christian fold at a single time, they seldom grasped or heeded Christian precepts. St. Eloi, for example, manifestly had his work cut out for him as mentor of the lusty King Dagobert I of Frankland, a ruler with three wives and more than a dozen concubines. The strenuous preachments of Eloi, Boniface and other great messengers of the Gospel survive to this day as evidence of the dubious mores with which they had to contend.

Other challenges also confronted the Church. The barbarian leaders infinitely preferred the pleasures of war and the hunt to the pain of desk work, whether involving the administration of a vast region, a duchy or merely of a district. The Church set itself the tasks of providing a variety of social services—relief for the poor, care of the sick and helpless, hospitality for travelers—and of mitigating violence through its teachings. Between the administrators supplied to the temporal powers, and those required for its own burgeoning affairs, the Church in time developed a continent-wide bureaucratic network of enormous power; its headquarters, the papal chancery, became the biggest and busiest office in Europe.

The backbone of this bureaucracy was supplied by the clerics, or clerks—men who, in preparation for ordination as priests, had taken one of the four minor religious orders: doorkeeper, reader, exorcist or acolyte. Actually, many never went on to the priesthood; nonetheless they enjoyed a number of valuable privileges, including immunity from trial by temporal courts and from the requirement to do military service. In return they put at the disposal of the Church the one skill they had in common—a rare one in that unlettered period—the ability to read and write. The clerics were the prototypes of today's civil servants.

Friction between church and state was minimal in these early centuries; there was room at the top for both. Aware of their interdependence, temporal and spiritual powers operated on a practical basis of *quid pro quo*. It was with the sanction of Pope Zachary that Charlemagne's father, Pepin the Short, ousted the last of the Merovingian kings and ruled in his stead. St. Boniface himself anointed Pepin with holy oil—and also persuaded him to regularize his liaison with his Queen, Bertrada, thus legitimizing their son. In gratitude for papal backing, Pepin came to the defense of Pope Stephen III, Zachary's successor, against the Lombards of northern Italy, a recurrent threat to the safety of Rome. He also presented Stephen with the lands wrested from the Lombards. This gift, called the Donation of Pepin, was the origin of the papal states south of the Po River in central Italy, territories over which the Pope enjoyed temporal as well as spiritual sovereignty. (The sole vestige of them today is the 108.7-acre area of Vatican City.)

Charlemagne's relations with the Church were even closer-knit, and again to the benefit of both. He gained by conducting his conquests of Europe under the banner of Christianity; the Church gained by a royal ordinance ordering the Saxons—the largest and most perverse of the tribes he vanquished—to accept baptism or die. Charlemagne's motives in furthering the Church were not, however, wholly self-seeking; he genuinely hoped to make a reality of the ideal Christian world commonwealth propounded in the Fifth Century by St. Augustine, the greatest writer among the early Church Fathers, in his celebrated *City of God*.

Charlemagne built chapels and monasteries as energetically as he built fortifications. He was also addicted to discussing theological fine points. He affected the entire course of Church history by suggesting that the word *filioque* ("and from the Son") be added to the official Nicene Creed in order to

ECCLESIASTICAL OBJECTS, *such as the gilt copper and enamel pyx (above) and crosier (below), were skillfully and symbolically wrought by medieval craftsmen. The pyx, used to hold the Eucharist, became a dove; this crosier depicted the Annunciation.*

explain that the Holy Spirit proceeded not only from God the Father but equally from God the Son, Jesus Christ. The Pope accepted the inclusion with a reluctance that proved justified, for it was this doctrine that brought eventual formal schism between Latin and Greek Christians.

However smooth the partnership between Pope and king, the very fact of their interdependence boded ill. Pepin's anointing with holy oil established him as ruler "by the grace of God." By threatening to withhold this rite from later monarchs, later popes could, in effect, determine the legitimacy of a head of state. Charlemagne's coronation by Pope Leo III established him as Western head of the Roman Empire. By this act of papal initiative, Leo's successors could claim that it was the papacy that had transferred the old imperial line from east to west, and the papacy therefore that had final say over the disposition of the crown.

The church-state dispute simmered in the renewed anarchy that befell Europe after Charlemagne's death, but not until the 11th Century would it reach the boiling point. In the interim, other matters added fuel to the fire—matters born of human frailties and lusts, and also originating in the feudal system itself, which achieved its peak in the Ninth and 10th Centuries.

With the breakup of Charlemagne's empire into disordered fragments, the great feudal lords came into their own. Land was their power. In bestowing it, they could exact fealty in return. The recipient of such a holding became the lord's vassal, subject to his dictates. When the recipient was a bishop or abbot—as sometimes happened—he accepted a divided allegiance, simultaneously owed to his ecclesiastical superiors and to the lay donor. (Essentially the same dilemma is faced by Christian prelates in today's totalitarian regimes.)

The lay donor not only demanded this allegiance but asserted his right to choose the successor bishop or abbot when the incumbent died. His reasons were bluntly pragmatic. The churchman, being unmarried, had no heirs to whom to bequeath the lands he held. In the lord's view, these reverted to him to bestow again. Further, a vassal churchman had temporal as well as spiritual control over his lands, serving, in effect, as an official of the lord's government. Thus the lord deemed it his prerogative to decide who should govern within his domains, and to "invest" the chosen man with the office, even to conferring upon a bishop the ring and the crosier, the age-old symbols of his spiritual authority. Although a lord might still permit the traditional elections in which the clergy of a diocese chose their bishop, and the monks of a monastery their abbot, he could also withhold, from a choice he disapproved of, the lands of the bishopric or abbey.

The spreading practice of lay investiture gave rise to an evil equally abhorrent to Christian morals: simony, the buying and selling of Church offices, so called after the scriptural Simon Magus, the magician who tried to buy from St. Peter the power to confer the Holy Spirit. The trafficking was two-way. For a suitable sum, an influential churchman would sell a wealthy noble a Church office he wanted for his brother, cousin, nephew or ally; or the layman, in turn, would sell an ambitious cleric a bishopric or abbey. The emoluments to be derived from holding a lofty Church office, and controlling the income from its lands, drew many a covetous eye; and if an aspirant to a bishopric had to pay heavily for his post, he could retrieve the cost by demanding installation fees from his priests in turn. Seeping downward through the ranks of the clergy, cynicism and demoralization encouraged yet another evil. By the Ninth Century, clerical chastity and even celibacy had become a mockery; monasteries were permitting women hangers-on, and the numbers of priests and deacons who took wives or concubines had increased.

The low estate to which the Church sank by the Ninth Century was reflected in the words of men high in the hierarchy. Flaunting his simony, one bishop openly boasted: "I gave gold and I received the episcopate, but yet I do not fear to receive it back if I behave as I should. I ordain a priest and I receive gold; I make a deacon and I receive a heap of silver. . . . Behold the gold which I gave I have once more unlessened in my purse." Another simoniacal churchman, one Manasses, gave it as his opinion that it would be quite pleasant to be Bishop of Rheims "if one were not obliged now and then to sing Mass." Many bishops and abbots found tending their flocks more arduous than hunting, or fathering offspring, or partaking in the ceaseless small wars which marked the times. The lesser clergy followed suit. Dispensing services and charity to the poor became a bore; the priestly obligation to baptize or marry or bury a parishioner was now hedged about with demands for fees.

The papacy itself suffered deep degradation. It was bought and sold among a group of Roman noble clans, and at one point there were three men who claimed the office as of family right. The murder or poisoning of a pope of a rival faction was not uncommon; the average incumbency of a pope lasted for about three years. Some were, to say the least, of questionable character. Among them the most infamous was John XII, whose offenses included castrating dignitaries who displeased him, ordaining a deacon in a stable, setting houses on fire, appearing in public equipped with sword, helmet and cuirass, indulging in open love affairs and drinking to the health of the devil. After eight years in the papacy, John XII was deposed by a Church council convened in 963 by Otto the Great of Germany, the first monarch since Charlemagne to wield substantial power in Europe. Otto's action in ousting John and supplanting him with a pope of his personal choice may have been born of a northern sense of outraged morality, but it also arrogated to an emperor, henceforth, the right to confirm or reject an elected and consecrated pope, thereby further roiling the church-state waters.

Even as the Church began to seem hopelessly captive and entangled, however, voices were being raised on its behalf. Men of principle had watched with growing alarm the venality all around them. They saw the Church plunging toward extinction; the need to clean house was crucial. This task was spearheaded by a new monastic order, the Cluniacs, named after the abbey founded in 910 at Cluny in south-central France by Duke William the Pious of Aquitaine. The problem was gargantuan in scope. The papacy had to be rescued from the mire, monastery life had to be reformed, and the secular clergy had to be rid of such evils as lay investiture, simony, clerical marriage, concubinage and general sexual laxity.

Cluny's drive was immeasurably helped by its unique form of organization. Benedictine monasteries, being autonomous, were prey to local pressures; many had in fact fallen into evil ways. Cluniac houses were closely tied in one system. The parent house itself was an "exempt" abbey, under no obligation to lay lords or their creatures in the hierarchy, but responsible directly to Rome. For several centuries the Abbot of Cluny ranked next to the pope in ecclesiastical importance, and the monastic domain he ruled eventually included 300 far-flung priories.

The rise of Cluny canalized deep springs in Christendom. Everywhere men took heart from the attack on the abuses prevalent in the Church. The Cluniac order, moreover, was the one institution of its day wherein a talented peasant could still go as high as his ability would take him; it came to be staffed by a moral and intellectual elite. In short order, Cluniacs were sought after as bishops and archbishops. As its influence in the hierarchy grew, Cluny used the effective technique of infiltrating its partisans into the unreformed monasteries and the ranks of the corrupt secular clergy. Foes of reform did not easily yield; often the struggle was physical as well as spiritual. One hapless prior, for example, imposed by Abbot Odo of Cluny upon the monastery of Farfa, near Rome, was murdered by two monks who had been rivals for the office. Still, the great mission of cleansing and freeing the Church was launched.

While Cluny worked from the bottom up, Rome worked from the top down. Under an early reforming Pope, Nicholas II, a decree of 1059 put the election of future popes solely into the hands of the College of Cardinals. Next, the old Church position of papal legate, the pope's personal envoy, was immensely strengthened. Legates could go over the heads of the clergy of any diocese and make decisions in local matters regardless of the bishop's will; further, they were given the power to excommunicate, and to place an entire country under interdict—a complete halt of Church services and other ecclesiastical functions. The pope could thus make his presence felt in every corner of Christendom.

Clashes between the reformed papacy and the Empire now became inevitable. The conflict came to open warfare under the greatest of the reforming popes, Gregory VII. A Cluniac-oriented monk who had devoted his entire career to the reform movement, Gregory was a short, thin-voiced man who made up in fervor what he lacked in prepossessing physique. In 1075, two years after his elevation, he drew up the *Dictatus papae*, a memorandum addressed to himself and his staff which rocked medieval Europe to its foundations.

No ambiguity beclouded Gregory's words. He declared that the Church had been and always will be infallible, and that those disagreeing with it could not be regarded as Catholic Christians. The pope is supreme; he is "the only person whose feet are kissed by all princes." The pope's spiritual authority is absolute, and may never be questioned by anyone on earth. All secular powers owe him obedience; he can depose kings and emperors.

In the monumental tests of strength that ensued between church and state, the first great person-to-person encounter between pope and emperor grew out of Gregory's efforts to bring into line the fractious young man who then occupied the imperial throne, King Henry IV of Germany. At the time of Gregory's pronouncement, Henry was only 25, and of no mind to heed papal injunctions of any sort. Simoniacal elections suited him perfectly, and he detested papal interference in the choice of those he regarded as "his" bishops. In response to a papal reproof of his conduct—conveyed personally and in strong language by three envoys from Rome—Henry summoned a council of his captive German bishops, who declared Gregory deposed. Gregory responded by deposing Henry. At this point some of Henry's less admiring vassals, as well as the rebellious Saxons of his empire—a perennial source of trouble to him—invited the Pope to Augsburg, in Germany, to confer over the choice of a new king.

The Pope accepted and set out for Augsburg, stopping en route at Canossa, at the castle of his rich and powerful ally, the Countess Matilda of Tuscany. Here occurred one of the climactic moments of the long conflict between church and state. Henry was beaten and he knew it. With his wife and infant son, he hurried south across the Alps to meet the Pope. At Canossa, he was made to stand for three days before the castle's gates, in freezing cold, barefoot and wearing the humble wool garb of the penitent pilgrim. At the urging of the Countess Matilda, Gregory at last pardoned the abject ruler.

Over the ages Canossa would become a synonym for the Church at its most triumphant over the state. Actually it solved nothing. Despite his pardon from the Pope, Henry was still unacceptable to his German foes, who elected another king in his stead. Gregory, joining the forces against Henry, declared him "bound with the chain of anathema," pronounced him stripped of all royal power and ordered Christians not to obey his edicts. The struggle was not yet done. Once more gathering support, Henry again deposed Gregory and, going to Rome, there installed his own "anti-pope," Clement III. Gregory, broken in health, soon died. His last words were: "I have loved righteousness and hated iniquity; therefore I die in exile." Henry's victory, however, was transient. Rebellion dogged him for the remaining years of his life. By the time he died in 1106, the German nobles had deprived him of his throne, and given it to his son and jailer, Henry V.

There would be other encounters between popes and emperors, and other seesaws of power. Sometimes one would prevail, sometimes the other. There was a time when the Church triumphed, seeming almost to usher in a golden age of Christianity, but it was followed by a time in which the papacy was fought over, threatened, exiled and split three ways. The struggle between empire and papacy went on and on until the peoples of Europe no longer cared for either, and found that they could survive perfectly well with neither, or with a trio of popes and a brace of emperors. A new entity of power would rise up: the nation-state.

But before that point was reached, and in between the times of bitter conflict of church and state, there were times of peace and amity, when they worked together side by side. The most memorable of these was the period of the Crusades, when layman and churchman joined hands in a massive endeavor to recover the holy places of Christendom from the Moslem infidels.

THE DAY BEGINS *for a monk as he rises to pray about two hours before the dawn. The monks of medieval times got up even earlier—between 1:30 and 2:30 a.m., depending on the season of the year.*

COMMUNITIES OF PIOUS BRETHREN

Christian piety expressed itself in many ways in the 2,000 or more monasteries that dotted western Europe in the 12th Century. These communities represented more than a dozen orders, some of them sharply divergent in precepts and practices. Yet the various monasteries also had much in common: their daily routines and programs of worship had in some part been shaped by the Rule of St. Benedict. This monastic guide, written by Benedict of Nursia in the Sixth Century, remains to this day a model for most orders. Its basic regimen is illustrated here with photographs taken in a Cistercian monastery at Casamari, Italy.

TOGETHER IN PRAYER, *Casamari's monks (opposite) celebrate Mass before an altar wreathed in smoke from a censer. The medieval monks spent an average of five hours each day assembled in worship.*

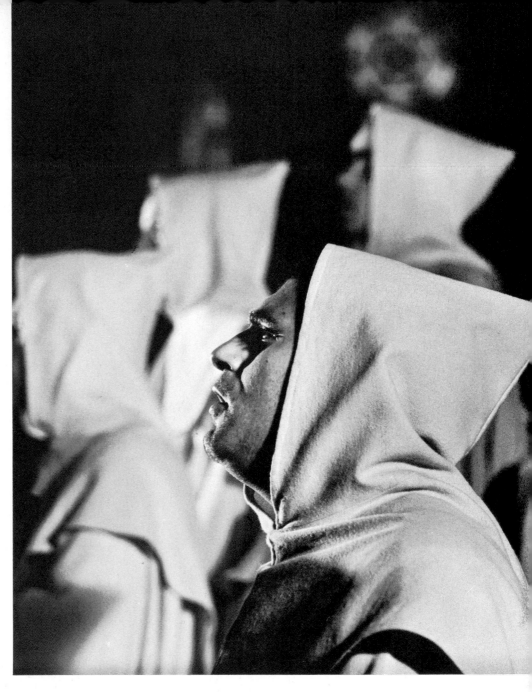

IN DEEP DEVOTION, *a monk raises his voice in God's praise. He wears the white habit that earned Cistercians the name "White Monks." Such details of dress as belts and long sleeves are marks of monastic rank.*

The Many Facets of Communal Worship

Liturgical prayer was the monk's chief activity, and in most monasteries it brought the brothers together nine times a day—for the eight Divine Offices prescribed by the Rule of St. Benedict, plus one Mass. However, each order adapted this program to its own purposes. The Cluniac order, a 10th Century outgrowth of the Benedictines, dedicated itself almost exclusively to communal prayer; its services went on day and night, sustained by three shifts of monks. In the 11th Century, monks who felt that this was excessive founded the Cistercian order, which returned to the brief, simple services described in the Rule. Even more austere was the Carthusian order, formed in 1084. The Carthusians assembled for only three offices a day; they completed their devotions alone in their cells.

Deliberations in the Chapter Hall

Each day, in every monastery following the Rule of St. Benedict, the monks met in the chapter hall *(above)* to conduct the spiritual affairs of the community. The abbot, their elected leader, sat in the most prominent place (the big chair at rear); the brothers flanked him in an order determined by seniority.

After a prayer, one monk *(foreground)* read a chapter (hence the name "chapter hall") from the Rule, whose full text was read aloud three times a year "so that none of the brethren may excuse himself on the ground of ignorance." Then the abbot might hold a remedial session in which each monk admitted his shortcomings. In meetings held strictly for business, the abbot often asked the brothers for advice on any special problem—as, for example, whether to accept an offer for an unused tract of monastery land. With all things put in order, a prayer concluded the meeting, and the day's work could begin.

TOILING AS FARMERS, *monks break the sod to plant vegetables. The monks of some orders were not obliged to do manual labor; monasteries which*

owned vast estates sometimes delegated all the field work to peasants.

Ingenious Variations
on a Tradition of Humble Toil

Most monks worked at manual labor for about six hours a day. In their work projects the monasteries often showed great enterprise. Some succeeded in bold experiments with swamp reclamation and forest conservation. A German abbey at Waldsassen developed one of the greatest fish hatcheries of its time. English Cistercians, endowed with tracts of hilly wastelands, specialized in raising sheep for wool. Their venture proved so lucrative that in 1198, when King Richard was held captive in Austria, the Cistercians were able to pay more than a third of the huge ransom demanded for his release.

DOING EXTRA CHORES, *monks sweep the church portico. Many brothers were skilled craftsmen: a monastery might have a miller, shoemaker, apothecary, beekeeper and even "master of fishes."*

"Fighting the Devil by Pen and Ink"

Scholarly pursuits were considered virtuous in the monasteries. Monks were granted free time each day for studying (*above*), and every encouragement was offered to manuscript copyists. The Carthusian monks were permitted to keep writing materials in their bare cells; Cistercian copyists were exempted from labor in the fields.

Completing a manuscript was arduous work: a single monk might spend well over a year copying the Bible. Several copyists described graphically the torments of writing all day for weeks on end—the bent backs, the aching muscles, the fingers numbed by winter cold. But for the copyists, writing was a way of "fighting the Devil by pen and ink," and all shared the hope of one scribe who declared: "for every letter, line, and point, a sin is forgiven me."

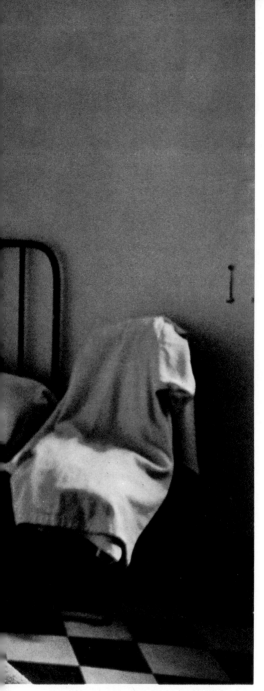

AT DIVINE STUDY, *a modern monk reads alone in his cell. As monastic learning flowered, one Danish abbey was founded in the hope "that therein men of prominent erudition . . . would compile the annals of the Kingdom."*

AT CONFESSION, *a monk and his brother confessor kneel in church. Private devotions, together with divine studies, occupied most monks for periods totaling about four hours each working day—as well as most of Sunday.*

A World Held Secure
by Discipline and Obedience

A PROCESSION OF BROTHERS *emerges from church, into darkness and silence, after the final Office of the day. The Rule decreed that from then until morning "no one shall . . . say anything."*

A PATTERN OF SHADOWS *at the end of the day, cast on a wall at Casamari monastery, shows the monks being blessed by their abbot (right) as they file past him on the way to their quarters.*

The monks' long day of prayer and work ended at nightfall with Compline, a solemn ceremony whose name was derived from the Latin word meaning "completed." On leaving the church *(opposite)*, the brothers hurried in silence to their quarters *(below)* and went directly to bed.

Compline was one of the many obligations prescribed in St. Benedict's Rule and adopted in some form by every medieval order of monks. Each order also forbade personal possessions, curtailed speech, practiced self-denial and selfless obedience. Today, though the monk's life has been modified by the centuries, these disciplines still preserve the monasteries as islands of piety in the secular world.

3

CONQUEST BY CRUSADE

Of all the wars men have waged, none have been more zealously undertaken than those on behalf of a faith. And of these "holy wars," none have been bloodier and more protracted than the Christian Crusades of the Middle Ages. Crusades preoccupied medieval man for some 200 years, from the close of the 11th Century to the close of the 13th. A great burst of fervor marked their start; disillusionment and disarray marked their end.

There were mixed motives behind the Crusades. Even the declared intention for which they were launched—to recapture Christendom's Holy Places in Jerusalem from the control of the Moslem infidels—was somewhat flawed: although Christian pilgrims were harassed by taxes, they were rarely barred from these shrines. Practical considerations also impelled the Crusades. The Church of Rome saw in them an opportunity to spread its dominion eastward to the sphere of its archrival, the Greek Church. The kings and feudal lords of Western Europe glimpsed the prospect of new lands and riches. Nobles hoped to find an outlet for the energies of obstreperous younger sons. The clergy hoped to find a dumping ground for troublemakers.

The Crusaders themselves had conflicting impulses. They were fully aware of certain rewards in crusading promised them by the Church, including remission of penance for their past sins and postponement of their debts. They could also be wanton and brutal. They raped and plundered fellow Christians and committed incredible atrocities on their Moslem foes, sawing open dead bodies in search of gold and sometimes cooking and eating the flesh—a delicacy they found "better than spiced peacock," according to a chronicler of the times. Nevertheless, an abundance of simple faith also moved the Crusaders—and a profound personal reverence for the soil that Christ had trod. The intensity of this emotion was later caught by Shakespeare in the words of that pugnacious English monarch Henry IV: "We are impressed and engag'd to fight . . . To chase those pagans in those holy fields, Over whose acres walked those blessed feet, Which fourteen hundred years ago were nail'd, For our advantage on the bitter cross."

The Crusaders recovered the Holy Places, but kept them for less than a hundred years. In the

A CRUSADER'S RETURN, *after 16 years of absence, is commemorated by this statue of the Count of Vaudemont and his wife, Anne of Lorraine. Though her husband had been given up as dead, Anne had refused to abandon hope.*

achievement of this goal, as in the dream of extending Western power to the East, the Crusades ultimately failed. When they ended, Moslem rule was entrenched in the lands where the battles had raged, the Byzantine Empire of the Eastern Christians was fatally weakened, and Europe was once again turned inward. But it would never be the same; its windows on the world had been unshuttered, and every facet of medieval life affected.

So sweeping a change could not have been foreseen when the Crusades began. Their immediate cause was a military threat to the Eastern bastion of Christendom, Constantinople, the proud city founded by Constantine, the first Roman Emperor to become a Christian. Constantine's successors on the throne of Byzantium had had to cope with all sorts of Asiatic invaders; the Byzantines called them *Sarakēnos*, Easterners, and the word "Saracen" came to conjure up a warrior of fanatical fighting skill. The latest and by far the fiercest of these intruders—and devout Moslems besides—were the Seljuk Turks. In 1071 they routed thousands of Byzantines at a battle near Manzikert, beginning a drive deep into Asia Minor in which they stripped Byzantium of more than half of its realms.

In 1073 the Byzantine Emperor, Michael VII, appealed to Western Christendom for help. The desperation of his move may be gauged by the fact that only 19 years earlier the Eastern Church and the Western Church had split asunder in a climactic quarrel over doctrine. The schism notwithstanding, Michael dispatched envoys to Pope Gregory VII. Gregory was cordial, but he had his hands full at home fighting foes of Church reform.

Over the next quarter-century the Seljuk Turks continued their encroachments, seizing, among other strategic points, the ancient fortress of Nicaea, from which they were no more than a jump across the Straits of Bosporus to Constantinople. Another plea went out from another Byzantine Emperor,

Alexius Comnenus, to another Pope, Urban II. Alexius was shrewder than Michael. In his message to Rome he stressed not the danger to his crown but the mutual need of the faithful, West and East, to drive the Moslem interloper from territories traditionally Christian.

Urban's response came at a Church council in November 1095 held at Clermont in southeastern France. The convocation glittered with cardinals and bishops and nobles. Lesser folk crowded the plain outside the church. After ecclesiastical matters were attended to, Urban moved outdoors, for he wanted the broadest possible audience for what he was about to say. He began, according to one version, by saying: "It is the imminent peril threatening you and all the faithful which has brought us hither. From the confines of Jerusalem and from the city of Constantinople a horrible tale has gone forth . . . an accursed race, a race utterly alienated from God . . . has invaded the lands of those Christians and has depopulated them by the sword, pillage and fire." Urban then enumerated the Turks' foul deeds, among them the ravage of churches or their use for Moslem rites, the defiling of altars, the rape of Christian women, and the torture and murder of their men. He spared no detail. One Turkish technique with victims, he reported, was to "perforate their navels, and dragging forth the extremity of the intestines, bind it to a stake; then with flogging they lead the victim around until the viscera having gushed forth the victim falls prostrate upon the ground."

Urban proceeded: "On whom, therefore, is the labor of avenging these wrongs and of recovering this territory incumbent, if not upon you? . . . Enter upon the road to the Holy Sepulcher; wrest that land from the wicked race, and subject it to yourselves."

There were many more words, for artfully mingled with the appeal to passion was an appeal to

A SEASON OF DEFEAT *is described in this letter sent in 1220 from the embattled bishops of the Holy Land to King Philip Augustus of France. The letter, bearing the wax seals of the nine signatories, recounts the distress caused by strong Saracen raids.*

practicality. Urban reminded his listeners that the land to which they would be going "floweth with milk and honey . . . like another paradise of delights," whereas the land they would be leaving was "too narrow for your population" and notably poor in food resources. To a France suffering widespread famine that year, the point was a telling one.

As Urban ended, a roar rose from the multitude: "*Deus volt! Deus volt!*" (God wills it!). If this thunderous spontaneity exceeded expectation, the Pontiff proved equal to it. Right then and there he declared that *Deus volt* would be the battle cry against the foe, and that each man embarking upon the sacred venture was to wear the sign of the Cross upon his mantle or cassock or tunic. Fulcher of Chartres, who was present, joyfully recalled: "O how fitting it was, how pleasing to us all to see these crosses."

Before the assemblage adjourned, many in it had ripped their cloaks for strips of cloth to place crosswise upon themselves. The gesture was soon to be repeated by scores of thousands throughout the West. Men now experienced the impact of propaganda skillfully and assiduously disseminated. Added to the spoken exhortations by priests and preachers were all manner of written tracts elaborating on the Moslems' odious behavior. Even the graphic arts were exploited. Depictions of a monstrous Turk trampling the Cross were circulated from village to village.

Fortuitously, the propagandists could also capitalize upon a mood of genuine piety born of Church reform the century before. Many people had been moved to escape their insular lives and go on lengthy pilgrimages to the tombs of St. Peter in Rome, St. James in Compostela and St. Mark in Venice; many had traveled to the Holy Land.

Combined with the pilgrimage ardor, the propaganda roused Western Christendom to fever pitch. While Urban and the aristocrats were planning an official expedition, the plain people surged forth on their own. One of history's more bizarre figures was responsible for this peoples' Crusade. He was Peter, a hermit of Amiens, who might well have fitted in among the ancient prophets. His hair was wild, his eyes rolled, and his speech was torrential. His hypnotized listeners in the marketplaces, convinced that he was more than mortal, plucked hairs from his mule's tail to keep as holy relics.

As a firebrand, Peter was unexcelled. Peasants all over France and the Rhineland flung down their tools. Soon two French and three German contingents began streaming toward the Danube Valley. This ragged host, numbering perhaps 50,000, included entire families with small children who, as each new town was reached, would plaintively ask whether this was Jerusalem.

Among the Germans, the obsession to kill the infidel found vent even before the marchers left their own land. The Jews of Speyer, Mainz, Worms and other towns provided a ready target. When the Archbishop of Cologne gave thousands of them sanctuary in his palace, attackers axed down the doors and massacred the lot. Farther east, the peasant Crusaders cast enraged eyes on the rich wheat stores of Bulgaria and decided that the Bulgars, too, were heathen. But after they had endured carnage and spoliation, the Bulgars struck back. They slew the Westerners as they slept by their campfires, or poisoned the wells en route with the rotting carcasses of sheep.

Sickness and exhaustion also took a toll. Only a remnant of the original starters reached Constantinople, arriving in the late summer of 1096. The Emperor Alexius beheld the ravening survivors and prudently shipped them across to Asia Minor, where the Turks mowed them down wholesale.

If the Crusade of the people ended in tragedy, the First Crusade of the princes ended in triumph. By early 1097, four expeditionary forces converged on Constantinople by land and by sea. Among them were Frenchmen, Provençals, Flemings, Germans, Sicilians and, most redoubtable of all, Normans. Rovers and fighters by instinct and choice, these descendants of the Norsemen had under William the Conqueror taken over England just 30 years before, and more recently had driven the Saracens from Sicily. By the end of 1097 the crusading armies had recaptured Asia Minor for Alexius and had struck southward to win for themselves the major cities of Edessa in Armenia and Antioch and Tripoli in Syria. On July 15, 1099, after a five-week siege, came the ultimate victory: Jerusalem. In a ferocious climax in which the streets ran red with infidel blood, the Crusaders wrested the city from the Turks. At nightfall their hands were still bloody when they folded them in prayer and knelt at the Holy Sepulcher, "sobbing for excess of joy."

Romantic imaginations have ever since endowed the men of the First Crusade with a glamor not wholly deserved. Of their bravery in battle, there can be no doubt. The names of their leaders—the Norman Princes Bohemond and Tancred, Godfrey of Bouillon and his brother Baldwin of Boulogne, Raymond of Toulouse—constitute a roll call of valor. But certain hard facts detract from the idealized picture of the Crusaders as great, hulking warriors in burnished armor astride splendid steeds, mailed fists ready at sword's hilt or at brilliantly pennanted lances. The average knight stood about five foot three inches tall. His horse, the ancestor of the modern Percheron draft animal, may have been splendid, but it was hardly spirited. The shining armor of the knight was another figment of fancy. This rigid, iron-plated uniform did not evolve until after the Crusades. Instead the knight wore a hauberk, a leather or linen coat to which were sewed many small iron rings as a protective sheath.

Away from combat, the Crusaders were hardly models of propriety. The citizens of Constantinople

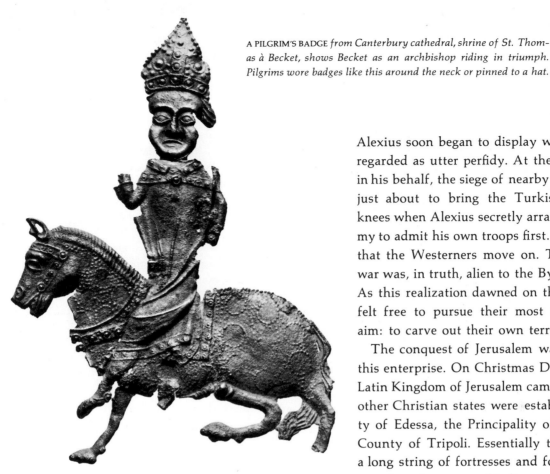

A PILGRIM'S BADGE *from Canterbury cathedral, shrine of St. Thomas à Becket, shows Becket as an archbishop riding in triumph. Pilgrims wore badges like this around the neck or pinned to a hat.*

detested their cloddish ways. Even among the more urbane Westerners the city stirred slack-jawed wonderment. At the time, Paris, London and Rome were little more than swollen market towns. Constantinople had paved streets lighted at night, colonnaded shops, parks, theaters, a hippodrome, mansions for the rich, blocks of workers' dwellings, the incomparable church of Hagia Sophia, and an imperial palace replete with marble, mosaics, gems and sumptuous fabrics. The city's wealth was tempting, and the Crusaders did not repress the urge to loot and pilfer. Anna Comnena, the Emperor's daughter and possibly the sourest female ever to put pen to paper, branded the newcomers as towheaded brutes "always agape for money."

Her father felt equally ill disposed. Scenting danger in the hordes that descended upon him—about 50,000 men in all—the Emperor extracted an oath of allegiance from their leaders and a pledge to accept his overlordship of all lands they would take. But

Alexius soon began to display what the Crusaders regarded as utter perfidy. At their initial operation in his behalf, the siege of nearby Nicaea, they were just about to bring the Turkish garrison to its knees when Alexius secretly arranged with the enemy to admit his own troops first. He then suggested that the Westerners move on. The idea of a holy war was, in truth, alien to the Byzantine mentality. As this realization dawned on the Crusaders, they felt free to pursue their most cherished military aim: to carve out their own territories in the East.

The conquest of Jerusalem was the capstone of this enterprise. On Christmas Day, 1100, the new Latin Kingdom of Jerusalem came into being. Three other Christian states were established: the County of Edessa, the Principality of Antioch and the County of Tripoli. Essentially the four comprised a long string of fortresses and fortified ports along a strip of eastern Mediterranean coastline. In Europe the states were known collectively as Outremer, the land "beyond the seas."

For almost 200 years Outremer was to be Western Christendom's toehold in the East. Two sources of strength sustained it. The Italian shipping cities of Venice, Genoa and Pisa served as a lifeline providing supplies and recruits. In Outremer itself, the garrisons were defended by two new religious orders: the Knights Hospitaller and the Knights Templar (so called after Solomon's Temple in Jerusalem). The young blue bloods who formed the bulk of the membership functioned as soldier-monks. Accountable only to the Pope, they could and did go over the heads of Outremer's temporal leaders, sometimes even making treaties with the Moslems.

While negligible in expanse, Outremer had a profound impact on the thinking of Europe through the medium of the men who settled it. The first jolt Outremer's pioneers got was to realize that they disliked and were disliked by their fellow Christians, the Byzantines. The second was to realize

AN ERA OF AFRICAN ACHIEVEMENT

When the nobles of Europe ventured forth to take part in the Crusades, they were astonished to encounter, in a far land, a culture in many ways ahead of their own. The fact is that during the Middle Ages, there were many civilizations which flourished unknown to most Europeans. For instance, in the 13th Century the Yoruba tribe of West Africa was achieving a high degree of artistic sophistication. The bronze at left, a representative example, is thought to depict the divine King of the Yoruba, the Oni of Ife. Ife was the religious center of Yorubaland—a large sector of what is now southwestern Nigeria. An urban people, the Yoruba founded a number of city-states whose rulers were subject to the supreme king at Ife. In this ordered society, art bloomed. Master sculptors carved in ivory or cast remarkably realistic statues in bronze for the royal court.

that they really rather liked the Moslems, especially in the frequent periods when they lived side by side in amity.

If the Moslems' conduct was a revelation, so were the niceties of their way of life and even the languorous sunshine in which they dwelt. Coming from a society where windows were slits that let in more cold than light, where clothes and bodies rarely were washed, the Westerners were overwhelmed. Among the domestic delights which they quickly embraced were Persian carpets, brocaded wall hangings, furniture inlaid with mother-of-pearl, and wide windows that looked out over flower-filled gardens to blue seas. And there was more: running water in pipes, Roman sewers that still worked, excellent medical services, and agreeable medicaments made of rose jam and spiced cream rather than cat's grease and stewed slugs.

As the cleric Fulcher of Chartres summed it all up: "He who was a Roman or a Frank has . . . become a Galilean or Palestinian. . . . We have already forgotten our birthplaces." The break with the past was so sharp that when a Second Crusade came along in 1147, its crashing failure was blamed on Outremer's tepid response. The new Crusade was provoked by the fall of Edessa, Outremer's northern outpost, to a forceful Moslem chieftain from neighboring Mosul, Zengi, who aimed to infuse new vigor into the disunited Moslems of the coastal areas. The men of Outremer seemed merely irked at this threat to their tranquillity. But their Christian brethren back home, fearful that Islam was once more on the march, erupted.

The Second Crusade was marked by the personal participation of two monarchs, Louis VII of France and Conrad III of Germany. The feat of recruiting them was effected by the most celebrated church-man of the times, Abbot Bernard of Clairvaux. Bernard was to the Second Crusade what Urban II had been to the First: its vital spark. He was a Cistercian, one of the more austere monastic orders founded in the wake of Church reform. Although he had renounced the world, his powerful intellect and his relentless defense of orthodoxy had made him counselor of popes and kings. When he fixed his blazing blue eyes upon Conrad and talked of the terrible Judgment Day awaiting those who failed to take up the Cross, the Emperor of Germany had no choice. Bernard never minced words. Acknowledging that all but a few in the ranks of the new Crusaders were thieves, murderers or perjurers, he nevertheless hailed their departure: "Europe rejoices to lose them and Palestine to gain them; they are useful in both ways, in their absence from here and their presence there."

Despite Bernard's rhetoric and the presence of royalty, the Second Crusade achieved nothing. Its armies did not even try to retake Edessa. After two futile years the Crusade melted away. Its major significance lay in certain side journeys made prior to the arrival in the East. En route, English and Flemish Crusaders stopped off to capture Lisbon from the Moors. Saxon and Danish contingents detoured across the Elbe, into what is now East Germany, to conquer the heathen Wends. A papal announcement that the Eastern venture counted as a Crusade astounded and disillusioned the European Christians, to whom crusading was synonymous with the deliverance of Jerusalem.

Cynicism also appeared in another guise. The papacy needed money to meet such obligations as the providing of legates for the new Christian lands in the East. The Church began to sell indulgences which remitted in part or in full the pain that sinful souls would suffer as penance in purgatory. At first, Crusaders bought or earned these indulgences

for their deceased families and friends. Later, a money payment could obtain release from the obligation to go on a Crusade at all. A man might take the Cross but pay someone else to go, or he might give a specified sum to the Church which would then, in theory, purchase a substitute.

The spread of this practice underscored a drastic change of attitude toward the Crusades. People began to regard them as irritating interruptions of life, or, alternately, as undertakings too dangerous for liking. They had good reason for this view, for disaster increasingly dogged these ventures.

After the fiasco of the Kings in 1149, there were six more major Crusades and many minor expeditions. But never again would the success and spirit of the First Crusade be duplicated. The Third Crusade came nearest to it in rousing popular furor. In 1187 the forces of a great new Saracen leader, Saladin, a man of enormous courage and character, captured Jerusalem in an openly avowed *jihad*. This counter-Crusade shocked Europe to its core and brought its three most powerful rulers to the East: Frederick Barbarossa of Germany, Philip Augustus of France and Richard the Lionhearted of England. But they availed nothing. Frederick drowned in a cold mountain stream in Asia Minor, and Philip went home. Richard, in time, concluded a pact with Saladin which reduced the Latin Kingdom to a coastal strip from Tyre to Jaffa.

Perhaps best remembered about this Crusade is the gallantry which Richard and Saladin displayed toward each other in the midst of otherwise brutal dealings. Saladin had the edge in this regard. Battling Richard at Jaffa, for example, he learned that the Englishman's horse had been killed under him; promptly he sent a groom leading two fresh mounts. He also allowed the Christians of Jerusalem, for a price, to leave the city with all their possessions, and he permitted them to continue to visit the Holy Places freely—if they came unarmed.

The Crusades that followed the Third were increasingly unrecognizable as such. Pope Innocent III—by far the most vigorous exponent of papal power in all the Middle Ages—personally preached the Fourth Crusade, yet it never even reached the Holy Land. The wily Doge of Venice diverted it to frankly commercial ends. Venetians and Crusaders combined to seize a rival port city in Dalmatia, Zara, which was populated entirely by Christians. Then, for good measure, they went on to besiege and sack Constantinople in 1204. Whatever ties remained between Eastern and Western Christendom were breached. The papacy itself, unable to exert control over the whole sordid venture, lost face.

Eight years later, in 1212, came a pair of incredibly pathetic children's Crusades. A 12-year-old French farm boy, Stephen of Cloyes, insisted that Christ had appeared to him while he was tending his sheep and had bidden him organize a children's Crusade to Jerusalem. While the grownups smiled, some 30,000 French youngsters heeded Stephen's call and with him marched through Provence to Marseilles. There they expected the Lord to part the waters for them, as He had done for Moses, so that they could walk dry-shod across the Mediterranean to the Holy Land. Slave traders lured them aboard ship and sold them to the Saracens of North Africa and Egypt. A Crusade of 20,000 German children, the same year, got no farther than Italy. Some, straggling back home, were forced into service by the peasants who had jeered their departure. Some of the girls ended up in Roman brothels.

In 1229 the strangest Crusade of all took place: a bloodless diplomatic Crusade by a monarch even then under excommunication by the Pope. The Emperor Frederick II of Germany, grandson of Barbarossa, was in every way extraordinary for his era. He was unusually well educated and spoke six languages, including Arabic; this intellectual achievement, among others, had earned him the label of *stupor mundi*, "wonder of the world." He was accused of being skeptical of Church dogma, and his persistent flouting of papal authority foreshadowed a new kind of independent secular statesmanship on the European scene. Frederick believed in negotiation. Arriving with his armies in the East, he had a congenial visit with the Sultan of Egypt, and without a single blow secured Jersualem, Bethlehem and Nazareth by treaty.

Frederick's victory for Christendom was, however, short-lived. The Saracens retook Jerusalem in 1244. Two subsequent Crusades by the saintly King Louis IX of France ended in his death from dysentery. In 1291 the forces of Islam took Acre, the last Christian bulwark in the Holy Land, and the Crusades, for all intents and purposes, were over.

Few in Europe mourned their end. The more amiable results of contact with the civilizations of Islam and Byzantium were everywhere in evidence. Venetians adapted the glassmaking techniques of Tyre. French villagers cultivated silkworms and wove lustrous fabrics in the tradition of the East. Farmers planted plum trees from Damascus and sugar cane from Tripoli. Cinnamon, cloves and nutmeg gave spice to European cookery. Women used glass mirrors in place of polished metal disks. Men relished the sensuous comfort of steam baths.

But far more fundamental changes were afoot. Feudal families were finding themselves reduced in means and in stature; to help finance their forays to the East, they sometimes had to sell charters to towns and freedom to serfs. The towns were now big and proud, and the new freemen assertive. The economy was no longer based on barter and services, but on money. Merchant princes had arisen to rival the feudal barons in prestige. Tradespeople and artisans prospered. The very structure of medieval society was in stress, its patterns of life in upheaval. The Crusades forgotten, new adventures on its own soil absorbed the West.

A MYSTICAL VISION *of man's nature and place in the cosmos is beheld by a German nun (lower left).*

PERILOUS JOURNEY OF THE SOUL

Most medieval people were illiterate and left no record of their beliefs. But the popular piety of the age can be seen clearly in various influences that shaped it and that still survive: Christian teachings, allegorical sculpture and verse, morality plays and mystical experiences such as the symbolic and complicated vision described by the nun Hildegard of Bingen in a 13th Century manuscript *(above)*. These evidences persuaded medieval man that the spiritual world was fully as real as the physical world; the chief importance of his mundane life was that its course would decide the fate of his soul. Each day, as he struggled between good and evil, his soul in its journey drew ever closer to heaven—or to hell.

A STEADFAST PILGRIM *faces three demons—Envy, "on all fours like a serpent." Treason, with a dagger in her teeth, and Slander, aiming a spear decked with ears.*

A SLEEK SEDUCTRESS, *Eve reaches out to pluck the apple that led to mankind's fall from divine grace. She is cupping her hand as if to whisper temptation to Adam.*

A World under Siege by Demons and Tempters

"Your life here is but a pilgrimage," declared the 14th Century poet Guillaume Digulleville, and illustrations of his work depicted as demons *(opposite)* the sins that imperiled man's soul on its journey. These creatures, wrote Guillaume, were "dreadful and horrible, And to behold full terrible."

But evil also took alluring forms. The Biblical temptress Eve, portrayed below by the master sculptor Gislebertus, was all the more dangerous for her beauty; a 12th Century morality play showed Eve working her fateful wiles on her mate, urging him, "Eat, Adam, wait no longer. Take this apple for your greater felicity." According to one distinguished preacher, even the saintly were suspect: the devil was so treacherous that he appeared in the guise of "apostles and angels and other saints and good men."

THE LADDER OF VIRTUE *is scaled by seven virgins seeking Christ's rewards (top) for an ideal life. In their ascent they spear the dragon of wickedness and escape a fierce pagan.*

Hopes and Prayers
for the Soul's Safe Passage

The childlike piety of medieval man reveals itself dramatically in the aids he adopted to fortify his soul on its hazardous journey. Imaginative but literal-minded, he personified the Christian virtues or conceived of them as the rungs of a ladder *(right)* that linked earth to heaven. He found reassurance in numbers. For example, 3 represented the spirit, 4 the body; their sum, 7, a mystical completeness.

In the popular imagination, man's greatest help came from Christ's mother Mary *(opposite)*. Ineffably human and merciful, the Virgin was considered to be always eager to intercede with her Son in man's behalf, to forgive sinners and to protect those in dire danger. Medieval man told many homespun tales about her. In one story, Mary saves a worshipful robber by supporting him for three days as he hangs on the gallows. In another, she takes a knight's place and fights in a tournament while he attends church. Medieval man felt he could converse freely with divine figures, and several stories report their replies—in the accents of everyday speech. In one such tale, a clergyman who has been praying only to Mary receives a visit from Christ, who tells him: "My Mother thanks you much for all the Salutations that you make her; but still you should not forget to salute me also."

THE MERCIFUL MOTHER, *Mary carries her son Jesus on the flight into Egypt. Many childless women, including a queen of France, made long journeys on foot to pray for heirs at Mary's shrines.*

Everlasting Punishment for the Legions of Sinners

To medieval people, the Day of Judgment was always imminent, and its program was frighteningly familiar. At midnight on that terrible day, all souls would appear in bodily form before the Creator. Each would be weighed *(right)* so that, as Dante wrote, "by its merits or demerits it [would expose] itself to the rewards or punishments of justice." Sinners *(below)* would be consigned to hell, sometimes depicted as the mouth of a monster *(opposite)*. In the vision of hell seen by the nun Hildegard of Bingen, "some souls were burned, and others were girdled with snakes. . . . And I saw demons with fiery scourges beating hither and thither." Here, in torment, sinners would spend eternity.

THE SCALE OF JUSTICE *indicates the presence of a deserving soul by tilting toward the archangel Michael. The devil was sometimes shown trying in vain to weight the balance in his own favor.*

THE SOULS OF THE DAMNED, *in piteous postures of terror, are separated from the elect and are driven off toward hell by a sword-wielding angel.*

THE MAW OF HELL *swallows up both the damned and their tireless tormentors, and is then locked up forever by an angel (left).*

Souls of the Virtuous in a Realm of Light

What awaited the souls of the worthy in heaven? The artists' view was often highly symbolic *(opposite)*. Hildegard of Bingen wrote ecstatically: "I saw a most glorious light and in it a human form of sapphire hue . . . all inter-existent in one light, one virtue and one power." Said Dante: "I saw ingathered, bound by love in one volume, the scattered leaves of all the universe." To attain this realm—and to escape hell's torments—medieval man hewed close to the advice one mystic received from heaven: "Keep the commandments of God, and dispose thy living after the example of righteous men."

AT HEAVEN'S GATE, *the souls of the elect look forward to perpetual bliss. All mortals, according to a popular medieval belief, would be resurrected at the Last Judgment—and all would be aged 30, whatever their age at death.*

IN GOD'S KINGDOM, *the heavenly hosts (opposite) assemble in orderly array. At top, winged angels attend Christ, represented by the lamb. Below, ranks of saints and martyrs holding palms sing a paean to the Creator.*

4

A NEW URBAN CLASS

In their heyday, medieval towns had little of the charm that now enchants the 20th Century. Within their encircling walls space was a luxury for the few. Jam-packed wooden houses, each a potential tinderbox, sought extra room through upper stories jutting out over the street. The streets themselves were mere alleys, six to 10 feet across. Sewers were open and sanitation scant. The stroller had to dodge slops from above and swilling pigs below; scabrous beggars jostled him. Except when he raised his eyes to the Gothic grace of town belfry or church spire, signs of filth and disease assailed him everywhere.

One great good, however, redeemed the townsman's condition. The air he breathed might be foul, but it was also free. Unlike his country cousin, the serf on the manor, he could tipple as he pleased and voice opinions as he saw fit. Physically his surroundings confined him; emotionally they enlarged him. The inner man fed on the brawl and bustle of urban life. His milieu was, in fact, the seedbed of the social, political and economic change that was ultimately to transform the Western world from medieval to modern.

Other than the cities that had survived the old Roman Empire, most towns of the Middle Ages did not evolve before the year 1000. The rebirth of trade spurred their rise. Paradoxically, commerce with the distant East preceded trade on the local level. Constantinople served as the crossroads. The city had grown into a great metropolis which manufactured many of its own goods and merchandised still others. It was accessible, by overland caravan or by ship, from all directions.

Constantinople offered opportunity—to those ready to come and get it. For Europeans the time became ripe in the 11th Century, with the reopening of the Mediterranean after some 400 years of Moslem domination. The Norman conquest of the Saracenic invaders of Sicily, and the Spanish Christians' rollback of the Arabic invaders of their soil stripped Islam of its control points along the Mediterranean's northern shores. The seafarers of Venice, Pisa, Amalfi, Genoa, Marseilles and Barcelona could sally forth more freely. Despite the hazards of Moslem pirates and the lack of navigational aids, sailing ships of the West began to put in at Constantinople and other ports of the Levant. The

A BUSTLING STREET *in 14th Century Siena is crowded with signs of prosperity: people bearing provisions, mules laden with wool and a goatherd tending goats. Inside one building (left) a teacher harangues his class.*

THE SEA ROUTES of three major maritime powers, plus a network of land routes, provided vital arteries for the great flourishing of European trade at the start of the 14th Century. By then, merchant vessels from Venice (solid blue line) and Genoa (short blue dashes) linked Asia with the Mediterranean, the Mediterranean with Channel ports. To the north, the flow of trade was monopolized by the Hanseatic League (long blue dashes), comprised of shipping centers such as Danzig, Hamburg and Bremen, as well as inland mercantile centers—Dortmund on a land route, Cologne on the Rhine. Thus, while Italy brought in silks and spices from the East and exported its own textiles and glassware, northern cities prospered from their trade in Russian hides and timber, Baltic fish and grain, Flemish cloth and German iron. In mid-14th Century, wars and plague disrupted this trade circuit.

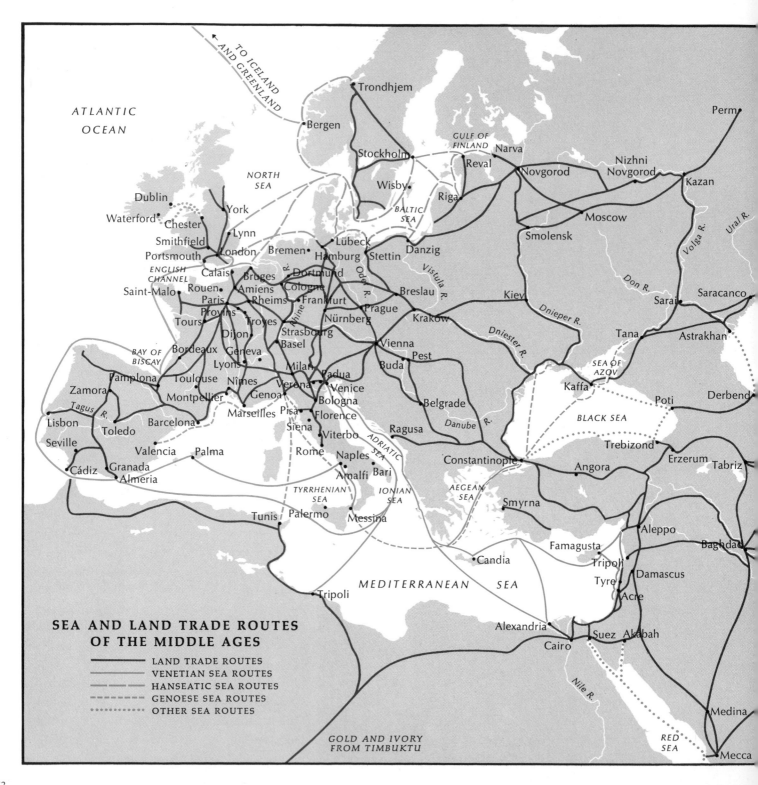

SEA AND LAND TRADE ROUTES
OF THE MIDDLE AGES

——————— LAND TRADE ROUTES
——————— VENETIAN SEA ROUTES
— — — — HANSEATIC SEA ROUTES
– – – – – GENOESE SEA ROUTES
·············· OTHER SEA ROUTES

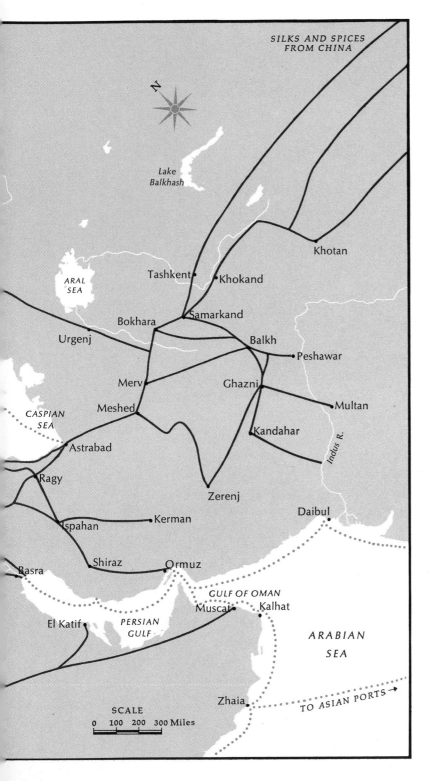

SILKS AND SPICES
FROM CHINA

Lake Balkhash

Khotan

Tashkent • Khokand

ARAL SEA

Bokhara • Samarkand

Urgenj

Balkh

• Peshawar

Merv

Ghazni

• Multan

Meshed

Kandahar

CASPIAN SEA

Indus R.

Astrabad

Ragy

Zerenj

Daibul

Ispahan • Kerman

Shiraz • Ormuz

Basra

GULF OF OMAN

Muscat • Kalhat

El Katif • PERSIAN GULF

ARABIAN SEA

SCALE
0 100 200 300 Miles

Zhaia • TO ASIAN PORTS →

stream of maritime traffic swelled with the Crusades, and with the resulting need to ferry men and supplies to and from the East.

All the enterprise of the traders would have availed little, however, without a coincident rise in the receptive spirit of the Europeans back home. After long hibernation, the Continent was once again astir. People were on the move, some on pilgrimages, others on their way to farming areas opened up by improved methods of agriculture. The change of scene invited a change of outlook, and Europeans became less wary of the unfamiliar. At the same time, as agricultural advance brought greater prosperity and a growth of population, they began to feel that life could hold more than the day-to-day skirmish for survival.

In this propitious climate the introduction of exotic wares from the East whetted appetites for more. Most of the imports were prohibitive in cost except for the rich—the noble intrigued by an intricate tapestry, the prelate seeking a gold chalice. But the foreign cornucopia contained plenties to which lesser people might also aspire, among them sugar and spice, fabrics and dyes. Men set to planning what they might proffer in exchange. They now had incentive to produce beyond their own needs.

Initially, Europe had only one item of manufacture to export: cloth woven in rural Flanders from wool sent across the Channel from England. For the rest, early West-to-East trade dealt in such basic commodities as grain, flax, fish, salt and wines. Later, from Germany and Scandinavia, came timber and hides; from Russia, via trading stations established by Germans in the north and Genoese in the south, came hemp and honey, furs and caviar.

Along the teeming waterfronts of Constantinople and Jaffa and Alexandria, voyagers from various parts of Europe learned not only of the East but of each other. They grew aware not only of goods to be had, but of processes by which they could be made. Out of the stimulation of contacts and ideas came an expansion both of local European trade and local European manufacture. The porcelains and precious stones of the East could only be admired. But its indigo and lacquer could be utilized; its silver and other metals could be worked; its silk and damask and velvet could be duplicated. Products and techniques multiplied. The mounting evidence appeared at Europe's traditional fairs. At the biggest of them, in Champagne, midway on the land route from Italy to Flanders, booths displayed copper pots, leather saddles, swords, armor, cutlery, anvils, whetstones, wooden tubs, carts and cart wheels, clothing and shoes and gloves—every item the result of native European skill.

As trading places the fairs were unique. The feudal lords who sponsored them (and collected a tax on sales) guaranteed safe-conduct through their regions by the imposition of a "fair peace." A large French fair of some weeks' duration would draw traders from Scotland, England, Germany, Spain, Italy, Constantinople, Syria, Armenia and Egypt. Then and there they could buy, sell and settle debts. The profusion of currencies proved no hindrance. English marks, *angevins* of Normandy, Savoyard *écus*, Westphalian groats, Venetian ducats, Florentine florins, Byzantine gold hyperperon, Moslem dinar—all went through the obliging hands of Italian money-changers who weighed and tested them and determined values. From the *banc*, or bench, at which they performed this ritual came the institution of the bank, even as varied banking practices stemmed from the initial service of money changing.

For all their advantages, the fairs could not wholly satisfy Europe's traders. Despite the "fair peace," and the more widespread "Truce of God" proclaimed by the Church, which banned private feuding on feast days and certain weekdays, travel was still perilous. Moreover, the fairs were seasonal. Increas- ingly, the merchant-wanderers desired stability. Out of this need came the towns.

Practical necessity dictated that a town be situated so that it was convenient to commerce—either on a watercourse or at a juncture of roads. But because of banditry and persistent feudal warring, a town also had to be comfortably close to defensive fortifications—those of a royal palace, castle, monastery or episcopal seat. Wherever these two requirements were met, the traders settled and put down roots. Before long, their ranks were augmented by the adventurous and the footloose: serfs fleeing bondage; itinerant harvest hands; professional soldiers; younger sons of the nobility who had no hope of a patrimony; manorial smiths, carpenters and leatherworkers seeking wider scope for their skills. The apparatus of urban life developed quickly. Alongside the merchant and craftsman, the butcher, baker and tavernkeeper provided their essential services.

The new urban class—set apart by its liberation from dependence upon the soil—also came to rely less and less on the old *burg*, or fortified place, which had provided the initial protection. The new towns began to build their own defensive walls —wooden stockades at first, later stone ramparts flanked by towers, and often wide enough to allow room for granaries, gardens and stables.

As the roster of town residents swelled, walls once regarded as ample enclosures turned out to be cramping. Town buildings soared upward; in some places the equivalent of today's anti-skyscraper ordinances had to be enacted. In Rheims, for example, no building could exceed the height of the eaves of the cathedral. Its archdeacon was instructed to keep a daily lookout from the eave windows to insure that any construction under way stayed at a point below his eye-level. But for all the problems engendered by the medieval town custom of self-containment, few towns were without walls; they provided a proud distinction over the smaller open village. Whenever old walls had to be torn down to make way for new streets and structures, other bigger walls would always be built. Like the concentric rings of a tree, the successive sites marked progress toward maturity.

Many of Europe's renowned cities, among them Hamburg, Frankfurt, Innsbruck, Bruges, Ghent, Oxford and Cambridge, started from scratch during the latter half of the Middle Ages, while urban centers already in existence, such as London, Paris, Venice, Genoa, Milan and Florence, mushroomed astonishingly. An ordinary town might have 2,500 inhabitants, a sizable town 20,000. London and Genoa boasted 50,000 each; the largest, Paris, Venice and Milan, more than 100,000 each. Even as these populations expanded, new settlements sprang up. Between 1100 and 1250 alone the number of corporate towns—those with written charters enumerating their rights—multiplied tenfold.

This huge increase reflected a new phenomenon, the sharpening political awareness of urban Europeans. Under the feudal system, the land on which the towns were built was held by some abbot or bishop, noble or king, who could exact a variety of obligations in return. As towns prospered, taxes and tolls on mercantile activity alone produced healthy revenues for the feudal lords. Some constructed towns themselves and offered special inducements to settlers. Patently the ruling classes respected the power of the new money.

Townspeople speedily perceived the bargaining leverage they commanded. Having tasted economic freedom, they now chafed at political and social restraints. They saw no need to have the lord's permission—as serfs did—to marry, to move about, to hold and dispose of property. They wanted to be shed of compulsory participation in the lord's military adventures. They wanted their own courts and their own laws. Ordeal by fire or water, or trial by combat seemed hardly suited to adjudicate matters of business.

To press their demands, inhabitants of a town would frequently form themselves into an association known as a commune. The cities of Italy, which had the longest memories of municipal freedom, sparked the communal movement. Later it spread to the north. Some communes were able to achieve their ends only by insurrection. Often, however, negotiations with rulers were amicable.

It would remain for later generations to advance their claims as inalienable human "rights." Medieval men were content to regard what they sought as "privileges" to be granted by their betters. Yet, the charter won by a so-called "privileged town" became, for many of them, a constitution of individual freedom and self-government. This document was treasured proof of the entity of the town, along with other tangible evidences such as a town belfry, a watchtower manned day and night so that its bell might be sounded in emergencies; a town hall, where citizens could assemble; and a town seal, to authenticate town acts.

Municipal autonomy thrived. Most towns had a town council, made up of representatives of business groups. The council levied taxes and market tolls, oversaw wall and road repairs, and founded charitable services. It also organized the provisioning of the town and maintained its militia—functions that sometimes overlapped. Since food supplies were drawn from the surrounding countryside, a quarrel between two towns over control of such resources would often result in bloodshed.

While the town council busied itself with its concerns, a separate tribunal administered justice. The judgments rendered by its members produced a whole new body of law concerning marriage and inheritance, liens and debts, and all manner of business disputes. Petty tricksters were likely to be sentenced to a stay in the stocks. Crimes of

passion and violence were punished by castration, amputation of limbs, decapitation or hanging. Executions were enthusiastically attended, and evoked all the satisfaction of a rousing morality play.

Yet the same man who could enjoy watching the brutal dispatch of an errant neighbor could unite with other neighbors in a solidarity seldom surpassed. From the start, the exigencies of medieval life had brought home the lesson that individual survival depended upon collective strength. Although the problems of physical survival lessened with time, the group instinct persisted. One manifestation was the commune, through which its members took on political muscle. Even as this common effort succeeded, economic muscle was gained through the organization of guilds.

There were two types of guild—those of merchants in general, and those of particular crafts. While their prime purpose was economic self-protection, the guilds created a tight-knit bond between members that went far beyond the economic. If a man fell ill, guild brethren were designated to look after him. If he grew needy or infirm, they were required to visit him regularly, bringing food and clothing purchased out of guild profits. When he died, all guildmen had to pray for his soul. Guild funds paid his debts, bailed him out of jail, dowered his daughter, financed his funeral and supported his widow. The guild furnished his social life in the form of guildhall banquets, saint's-day celebrations, pageants and processions. It also improved his manners. He could not, for example, attend guild meetings stockingless.

Merchant guilds evolved out of the practice of long-distance traders banding together in caravans to assure their safety en route. Journeying en masse, they were better able not only to stave off highwaymen but to win concessions on toll rates from the noble owners of the lands through which they passed. The manifest advantages of collective action

were then applied on the merchants' home grounds through guilds which soon began to dominate and regulate all commerce within a town. Only its members could buy, sell or manufacture goods in the town. Outsiders had to secure guild consent for access to the local marketplace.

In time, as specialized trades multiplied, the merchant guilds were supplanted by the craft guilds. Each craft boasted its own guild. The textile industry alone included guilds for wool, flax and hemp merchants, wool combers, spinners, two kinds of silk spinner, seven kinds of weaver, dyers, fullers, calenderers, shearmen, textile sellers and four kinds of tailor. The textile crafts were among several which welcomed women (the word "spinster" memorializes those who supported themselves by spinning). Other hospitable opportunities were afforded them by the brewing industry, launching the tradition of alewives and barmaids.

Within its own sphere, the craft guild pursued practices as monopolistic as those of the merchant guild. No townsman could engage in the craft unless he belonged to the guild. Only the products of guild members could be sold in the markets. But in return for this protective umbrella the craftsman had to submit to rigorous regulation. To learn the trade, he had to serve as an apprentice without pay for anywhere from two to 10 years, depending

upon the intricacy of the work (the goldsmith's craft took longest). During this period he had to live with, and unquestioningly obey, the master workman who taught him. He then became a journeyman and could hire himself out for a daily wage. But he could still work only for a master; he was not allowed to deal directly with the public. To reach the pinnacle of master, he had to pass an examination by the guild's governors. Usually he was required to fashion his "masterpiece"—some product that gave visible proof of mastery of his craft.

He could now set up on his own, manufacturing his wares in the back of his house, selling them in a shop at the front, employing apprentices as learner-helpers. But he was far from a free agent. Stringent guild regulations continued to guide his every move. Some were of obvious benefit. The superlative craftsmanship still observable today in Europe's medieval buildings—in the iron grillwork and the stained-glass windows of cathedrals, for example—was the result of guild insistence on standards of performance and quality. A shoddy article would be denied the guildhall seal of approval (whence has come the prestige of the "hallmark"). Guild inspectors were always on the prowl. Stout fines, or even expulsion from the guild, awaited a baker who cheated on weight or a pepperer who adulterated his product with ground nutshells.

Not all guild regulations, however, were designed to inspire a man's best. Since the guild's basic aim was to insure scrupulously equal opportunity for all members, competition between them was unthinkable. The guild forbade a member to keep longer hours than his fellows, employ more apprentices or pay journeymen better wages. Nor could he advertise or push his wares. Members of the same craft were likely to congregate in the same quarter; the Mercer Streets and Ironmongers' Lanes and Shellfish Rows of European cities today recall this practice. The medieval buyer in search of a particular article would therefore face a battery of shops with similar wares. The shop owner was not permitted to draw his attention in any way. Even a cough or sneeze invited guild penalty.

There was yet another means of dampening the competitive urge: price-fixing. No guildman could charge more than his neighbor, and what he could charge was decided by the guild. In setting prices, the guild took its cue from the Church. In the eyes of the Church, the profit motive was ignoble, and profit-seeking persons plainly were more concerned with this life than with the hereafter; the price of goods, therefore, should be merely enough to cover costs of material and labor. In time, however, the Church adjusted its views. Its great 13th Century philosopher, Thomas Aquinas, elaborated the concept of a "just price" to one that allowed the seller enough of a margin to keep himself and family in reasonable comfort.

The Church also eventually reconciled itself to another growing reality of Europe's economic life: the merchant's need to borrow money to finance long-term or long-distance undertakings, and his willingness to pay interest for its use. Usury, in the modern sense, denotes the charge of exorbitant interest rates; in medieval times the term was applied to the charge of any interest rate whatever. The Church constantly thundered against usurers, deeming them guilty of mortal sin. Yet no less a personage than Pope Innocent III candidly commented, in 1208, that if all usurers were banned from the Church, as required by canon law, all churches might well shut down.

Ostensibly moneylending was permitted only to Jews, who were barred from guild membership and the livelihood it afforded, and who were not regarded as subject to Church precepts. In actual fact, the money traffic between Christian lender and borrower thrived through a variety of circumventions of the usury ban. One such technique was to lend money for nothing, but charge "damages" for delays in repayment. In the mid-13th Century Pope Innocent IV sanctioned payment to a lender for the temporary loss of use of his capital. Gradually antiusury laws were repealed.

With the acceptance of the capitalistic spirit and its profit motives, the earlier guild philosophy of providing exactly equal economic opportunity for one and all could no longer prevail. The guild itself became rigidly stratified. Through limitations on the admission of apprentices, a ceiling was put on the number who could rise to journeymen, hence masters. The masters were thus transformed into an upper crust over a proletariat of less skilled or unskilled workers. At the same time, men of enterprising bent began to flout guild regulations. They hired as many employees as they chose, set their own work hours and charged the best prices they could command. Acquiring surplus capital, they could become bankers and investors in other people's ventures. As fortunes grew, the new moneyed class pre-empted the title of bourgeoisie, once applied to all inhabitants of a burg. In the medieval scale, this class formed the so-called third estate, ranking after the first estate, the clergy, and the second estate, the nobles. Below were the masses of ordinary workers and the peasants.

The power of the third estate—the middle class—grew steadily more formidable. Dependent upon bourgeois wealth for their revenues, kings gave the rich merchants a voice in their councils. The merchants, in turn, supported the central authority against the feudal lords' last-ditch struggle for supremacy, spurring the rise of the centralized nation-state. Yet the same merchants could also harass and thwart royal rulers. The powerful Hanseatic League, a merchants' confederation of some 70 German towns which virtually monopolized commerce on the Baltic and North Seas, had only to threaten a trade embargo to enforce its demands. When the King of Denmark tried to seize the Hanseatic town of Wisby, the League warred on him, won a treaty which gave it control of the herring trade, and thereafter dominated Scandinavian politics.

Even as the collective impact of the merchant class was felt, the imprint of individual entrepreneurs came to be discerned. Europeans marveled at the exploits of Marco Polo, the son of a Venetian trader, who ventured all the way to the China coast, served for 17 years as adviser to the awesome Mongol potentate, Kublai Khan, and returned to Venice in 1295, reputedly vastly enriched. Several decades after Marco, a onetime Florentine shop boy named Francesco Datini built up a business in arms and armor, went on to dyeing and cloth manufacture, ultimately turned to banking and the promotion of new companies, and ended with a fortune of 70,000 florins. Along with merchant-adventurers and merchant-princes, great banking families emerged. The Spini and Bardi and Frescobaldi in Italy, the De la Poles in England wielded enormous influence everywhere on the Continent.

Whether as bankers, business leaders or captains of industry, the affluent bourgeoisie changed the face of Europe. The clergy frowned on their capitalist strivings. The nobles despised and snubbed them as lowborn *nouveaux riches*. But the third estate could not be denied an ever larger place in the medieval sun. Having built fine mansions and clothed their wives in furs and brocades, the new men set their sights still higher. They wanted their sons to be educated. They wanted to be patrons of the arts. They wanted to beautify their cities. In increasing flow, their money went into the proliferation of schools, the collection of manuscripts, the commissioning of painters, the construction of cathedrals and plazas and public monuments. It was in large part through their wealth, and the vigor with which they dispensed it, that medieval civilization came to full flower.

A VARIETY OF SHOPS—*a tailor's (left), an apothecary's (right), a barber's (background)—attests to the busy life of a medieval town.*

THE TRADERS' BUSTLING TOWNS

During the barbarian invasions, when European society broke down into self-sustaining feudal units, the old cities lost most of their commerce along with much of their population. But by the 11th Century, the revival of long-distance trade was stirring up commercial activity at the local level. This process was set in motion by a new breed of traveling men, the professional merchants. When winter halted their journeys, they gathered in crude trading communities which soon grew into thriving towns. Countless people were lured to these settlements by new opportunities for work and profit, and by a freedom born of the trader's mobility. Within a century, these dynamic towns were pioneering such modern institutions as representative government, banking and capitalism.

Walled Burgs and Burghers

Many medieval towns took root beside a burg, or fortified place, situated on a river or seacoast. Here their merchant-founders were both conveniently based for trade and reasonably safe from marauders. Some burgs were small castles. Others were citadels as large as Carcassonne, whose mile-long

ramparts *(above)* still ring a broad hilltop in southern France.

Outside the burg, the mercantile settlers built a market and homes—and then enclosed their town, the new burg, in walls of its own. The people within these walls soon acquired a definitive name. To distinguish them from the knights, clerics and serfs who resided in old burgs or unwalled villages, the people of the new towns were called *bürgers* in German, burgesses in English, *bourgeois* in French. At first these terms embraced all economic levels. That they came to denote middle-class affluence was testimony to the new burgs' spectacular success.

An Annual Round of International Fairs

Merchandise was the lifeblood of all the towns, and it was distributed to local markets through great international fairs, a few of them older than the towns themselves. The six greatest fairs were held in rotation in France's Champagne region, whose central location made it a natural meeting ground. Early each year, precious wares and important merchants converged on the area from as far away as Egypt and Scotland. On reaching the fair site, each national contingent set up stalls in its own area. The Flemish displayed their woolen goods, the Spaniards their cordovan leather, and Italian bankers arranged loans and credit transfers. All groups were protected by the counts of Champagne; all adhered to a special mercantile law.

Busy weeks later, the fair closed and the traders moved on. Major wholesalers might journey on to famous fairs at Ghent, Leipzig and even Novgorod in Russia. But by mid-November every merchant, loaded with new wares, was hurrying home for winter business in his own walled town.

OPENING FOR BUSINESS *with a bishop's blessing, a fair offers merchants a wide choice of wares—and promises idlers a lively outing.*

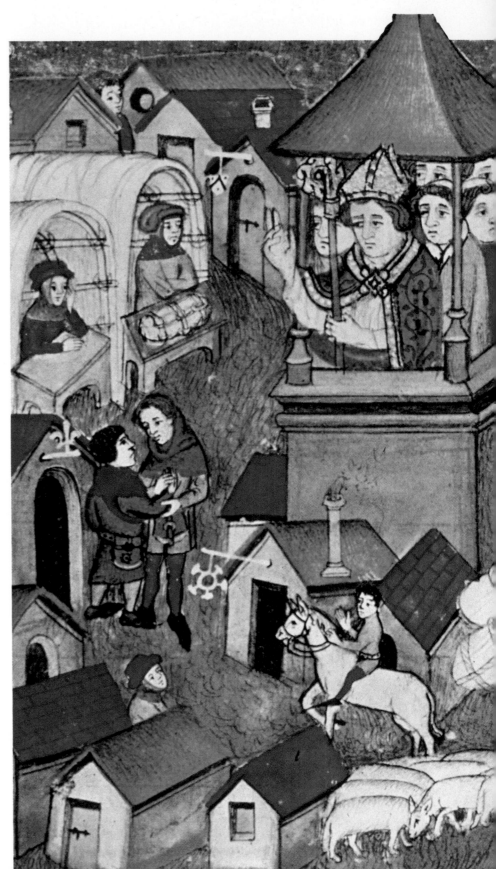

DEALING IN CURRENCY, *Italian bankers make change for coins—Byzantine and Arab as well as European. Their loan services were vital to the smooth flow of commerce in town and at fairs.*

TAKING ON MERCHANDISE, *a river barge loads at a Flemish port. Shipping was the cheapest and fastest mode of transportation. A merchant ship could travel 100 miles a day, a caravan 30 at most.*

SYMBOL OF THE GUILDS, *a regal figure oversees the work of a stone-mason, carving a capital, and a carpenter, drilling with an auger.*

GLASSMAKERS *stoke their furnace (right), shape the molten mass (center) and make sure that the final product (top left) meets guild standards.*

The Power of the Guild in Town Affairs

As the towns grew, so grew the guilds. These were voluntary protective associations formed by merchants and craftsmen; through their elected officials they worked to maintain the quality and price of local wares. One sign of their growing power was a monopoly granted to the dyers of Derby, England: "no one should dye cloth within ten leagues of Derby, except in Derby." As business expanded, the craft guilds proliferated. For example, Paris by 1292 had 130 "regulated professions," including medicine. By then the guilds had assumed many social functions—and even combined to run town governments.

TEXTILE DYERS *dip and stir long bolts of cloth. Under the watchful eye of their guilds, dyers and other craftsmen chose their apprentices carefully and put them through years of hard training.*

Chores and Joys of the Urban Life

For a well-to-do burgher, the day began with prayers at dawn. Then, braced by a draught of wine, he hurried off to work. Business took him on a familiar circuit of town—to the docks and the market to see to his merchandise, to the guildhall and the tavern to gossip about prices. He returned home for his first meal of the day at 10 a.m., and again for his supper at 6 p.m., and he ate his way through enormous repasts—including such fare as eels, roasts, black pudding, lark pastry, larded milk. His wife, besides preparing the food, kept house, managed the servants, tended the children and still found time to "have roses to grow . . . and make chaplets and dance and sing." Around 9 p.m. the members of the household turned in. With shutters bolted, they went to sleep "well bedded in white sheets . . . well covered with good furs, and assuaged with other joys and amusements."

IN A TAVERN, *tipplers are plied with drinks by the innkeeper, fancifully depicted in his cellar. Official ale tasters visited the taverns to approve the quality of each new brew. Many inns serving bad ale were closed down.*

IN A COMFORTABLE HOME, *an ailing burgher (opposite) takes a nap while his meal is prepared by his wife, at the fire, and her servant. A rich man's home might have such luxuries as carpets and glass windowpanes.*

A LEPROSY VICTIM *begging alms with a cripple, sounds his rattle to warn of his approach. The wandering lepers were admitted to most towns but were compelled to buy any object they touched.*

A GLOOMY ALLEY *poses health threats which were suffered in ignorance by its medieval tenants. Here—and in every cold, damp, malodorous street—respiratory diseases took an unrelenting toll.*

THE PLAGUE DEAD *receive a hasty mass burial at Tournai, in what is now Belgium, in 1349. The dread bubonic plague, known in its time as the Black Death, carried off about one quarter of Europe's population in seven years.*

Ordeals by Fire and Pestilence

Growing helter-skelter, medieval towns propagated the perils inherent in urban life. In their dense sprawls of wooden houses, built wall to wall along crooked alleys, a chance spark could easily spread and consume whole districts. London had four huge fires in the 12th Century, and Rouen burned six times between 1200 and 1225.

Towns were incubators of disease. Overcrowding, polluted wells, primitive sanitation, streets aswarm with pigs and rats—these bred typhus, typhoid and influenza. The worst of many epidemics, the bubonic plague, cut a terrible swath across Europe in the 1340s. Many French and German towns shared the fate of Venice, which lost three quarters of its population. "Grisly fury," said a medieval writer, "destroyed the principal cities of England." Everywhere, as in the town of Tournai (below), the survivors were hard pressed to bury their dead.

A LEGAL DECISION *is handed down in an Italian court. Three officials (rear) vote on appeals by rival litigants (right and left) while a notary, writing, commits the case to the town records.*

A Framework of Law for Precarious Times

In the 11th Century, towns began acquiring charters from kings and local lords. These documents officially granted rights that many towns had already assumed: to govern themselves, to enforce their own laws and taxes. Town law, administered by elected officers, covered every aspect of urban life. With crime rife in the streets, lawbreakers were mercilessly punished—hanged or decapitated (*right*) for robbery, flogged for minor offenses.

Yet the guiding spirit of town life was not one of cruelty. A new sense of local patriotism united the brawling townspeople; they built schools, hospitals and great churches—not only to meet their needs but to glorify their town. All were moved by a sentiment voiced in the charter of a Flemish town: "Let us help one another like a brother."

A PUBLIC EXECUTION, *the beheading of a highwayman, is carried out in 14th Century Paris. To the spectators, executions were a grim warning against crime—and also a stirring entertainment.*

5

ADVENTURES OF THE INTELLECT

In the course of every civilization a time comes when converging forces carry it to new heights. For the Middle Ages the time came in the 12th and 13th Centuries. Life itself was safer. The self-sufficiency of the town challenged the serfdom of the manor. Trading and crusading reaped unexpected harvests of sophistication. Increasingly, men found their vistas unshuttered. From a newfound base of physical and economic freedom they now embarked upon adventures of the intellect. In the process, the medieval mind and spirit were transformed, and the way was paved for the Renaissance.

Over this 200-year span, medieval civilization produced great contributions to culture that have survived to enrich each era since. Universities were founded. The beginnings of modern Western literature emerged. A philosophy of ethics ballasted the religion of revelation. Esthetic tastes were articulated in cathedral architecture, in fresco painting, in polyphonic music. Fresh breezes blew through the realms of political and scientific theorizing. Imaginative enterprise and speculative inquiry pervaded every endeavor.

The vital spark of this cultural explosion was the spread of education. In earlier medieval times, learning had been a privilege primarily enjoyed by the clergy. Benedict of Nursia, founding the Western monastic system in the Sixth Century, had bade the monks read and study; in response, Benedictine abbeys had developed a kind of rudimentary schooling in Latin and in the arts of lettering and illumination. Charlemagne, dreaming his ambitious dreams in the Eighth Century, had widened opportunities for scholarship through a decree that every monastery have a school to teach all those "who with God's help are able to learn." The Emperor himself set an example with a Palace School for his own children and those of his courtiers.

Even as the monastery schools taught candidates for the monastic orders, cathedral schools taught candidates for the secular clergy. But there was a crucial distinction between the two. Attached to the cathedrals, which were an integral part of town life, cathedral schools were more readily accessible to laymen. As more towns were established and more cathedrals were built, these schools proliferated throughout Europe, most notably in France—

MEDIEVAL ALLEGORY *is richly displayed in "The Lady and the Unicorn," a panel from a six-part 16th Century tapestry presented as a wedding gift. In this fanciful scene, the lion represents the groom, the unicorn his bride.*

at Tours, Rheims, Chartres, Paris and elsewhere. Among the students they attracted, a rising number came from the bourgeoisie and talented serfs.

The curriculum of the cathedral school was limited to grammar, rhetoric, logic, arithmetic, geometry, music and astronomy—the seven liberal arts, so called because in ancient Rome their study had been reserved for *liberi*, "freemen." Texts were provided by the writings of a few rare scholars of the early Middle Ages. One was Cassiodorus, a Sixth Century Roman whose two-part treatise, *The Handbook of Sacred and Secular Learning*, defined the liberal arts and interpreted the Bible. Another was Boethius, a contemporary of Cassiodorus, whose *Consolation of Philosophy*—written while he was in prison for an alleged plot against the barbarian King Theodoric—attempted to reconcile the misfortunes of man with the concept of a benevolent, omnipotent God. A third was Isidore of Seville, the Seventh Century author of *Etymologiae*, an encyclopedia on the liberal arts, medicine, law, theology, agriculture, war and many other subjects. A fourth was the Venerable Bede, a Benedictine monk of Eighth Century England, who produced a number of Biblical commentaries and treatises on theology and astronomy. These men, along with St. Augustine, Pope Gregory the Great and a few other Church Fathers, were known as *auctores*, "authorities," whose words the medieval student did not presume to contradict.

Learning was soon to be liberalized, however, with the advent of an era of great schoolmasters. The first of this new breed was Gerbert, master of the cathedral school at Rheims in the latter half of the 10th Century. The son of a serf, Gerbert was destined to end his days as Pope Sylvester II. But he left his mark upon history through an earlier circumstance. As a young monk, Gerbert had been so brilliant a student that his abbot had taken the unusual step of sending him to Spain to study

mathematics. Although Gerbert's mentor there was a Christian bishop, he was also exposed to the broad and tolerant culture of the ruling Moors.

A hundred years or so hence, after the Crusades began and Mediterranean commerce expanded, intellectual contact with Islam would become less and less of a rarity. Christian Europe would be introduced to Arabic medicine, astronomy, mathematics and philosophy. At Constantinople, as well as in Sicily and in Spain, Moslem and Jewish scholars would be kept busy turning out Latin translations not only of Arabic lore but also of ancient Hebrew and Greek writings they had preserved. Westerners would travel to the East to study the works of Aristotle in his own language. But this thriving traffic in knowledge was yet to come when Gerbert journeyed across the Pyrenees.

Gerbert brought back more than the news of a system of education so advanced that one center of learning at Cordova alone accommodated thousands of students. Of more lasting significance, he had absorbed the inquisitive, questing spirit of Moorish scholarship. When he began to teach at Rheims, he announced that the compilations of the *auctores* no longer sufficed; his pupils were henceforth to study Roman classics in the original. To this end Gerbert collected manuscripts wherever he could and built up a sizable library—no mean feat at a time when a manuscript sometimes took a year to copy, and cost at least the equivalent of a churchman's yearly income.

Out of the crop of superior students trained by Gerbert came Europe's next great schoolmaster: Fulbert, who became Bishop of Chartres and the driving force of its cathedral school. Fulbert's genius was as a catalyst, inspiring in his students a zest for dialectic—reasoning by argument. He and his successors at Chartres—Ivo, Bernard and Thierry—did more than fill their pupils' heads with information; they impelled them to express their ideas in their own words. Among them they taught many of the men who revolutionized thinking in 12th Century Europe.

The liveliest figure in this revolution, however, was a man who preferred to make his own rules: the celebrated teacher Abelard. Today Abelard is remembered chiefly for his poignant love affair with his pupil Heloïse. In his own time he was equally famous for his nimble wit and fearless tongue. The eldest son of a minor noble of Brittany, Abelard for love of learning had given up his inheritance rights to younger brothers, and roamed France to sit at the feet of the great masters, now listening, now openly challenging them in class. In time he established himself as a lecturer at Mont Ste. Geneviève in Paris, where he attracted a host of students. He also began to write.

In a treatise entitled *Sic et Non (Yes and No)*, he posed 158 questions on dogma and answered them with conflicting quotations from the Scriptures, the Church Fathers and pagan classics. "The first key to wisdom," Abelard asserted, "is assiduous and frequent questioning. . . . For by doubting we come to inquiry, and by inquiry we arrive at the truth." This idea, commonplace to the Greeks, was hardly so to medieval Europeans. Abelard's astounding opus won the applause of some, but alarmed as many others. Another of his books, on the nature of the Trinity, invoked condemnation by a Church council at Soissons in 1121, and its author was sentenced to confinement in a monastery.

Abelard was not a man to be kept down. A year later he secured the monastery's permission to leave and live in the wilderness southeast of Paris. Students flocked to his side. They built him a shelter, tilled his land and begged him to teach once more. Resuming his pursuit of reason, Abelard again and again fell afoul of conservatives in the Church, this time including Abbot Bernard of Clairvaux, the most influential prelate in Christendom. Ber-

A 13TH CENTURY SEAL *of the University of Paris illustrates the relationship between religion and medieval learning. The source of wisdom is divine, represented (at top) by the Virgin and Child, a saint and a bishop (left). At bottom, two professors teach.*

nard pursued Abelard as zealously as he preached the Second Crusade. "The faith of the righteous believes," he declared, "it does not dispute." At Bernard's instigation, a Church council at Sens in 1140 condemned Abelard for heresy. Abelard retired to the abbey of Cluny, where he stayed in seclusion for the remaining two years of his life.

Despite his condemnation, Abelard's method of inquiry persisted and flourished. By the 13th Century all Europe had a thirst for learning which ecclesiastical censure could not quench. Intellectual enterprise as a way of life thrived even in the shadow of that fearsome new institution, the Papal Inquisition. Established in 1233 to stamp out the Albigensian heretics of southern France, the Inquisition's courts of inquiry kept a sharp eye on maverick scholars as well. Nevertheless, the seeds that Abelard had planted in the medieval mind sprouted all around the Continent. Less than 100 years after his death universities thrived at Paris,

Orleans and Montpellier; across the Channel at Oxford and Cambridge; at Bologna and Padua.

The step that signaled the birth of the universities was the grouping of students and masters into guilds. As craftsmen had done before them, they banded together for mutual interest and protection, and called themselves a *universitas*, the medieval name for any corporate group. In Italy, where the majority of students were mature men pursuing advanced study in law and medicine, their guilds came to exercise great power. Students hired and paid teachers, determined the courses to be given, and fined any lecturer who skipped a chapter in expounding his subject. (Teachers at Bologna were even penalized for saving a difficult paragraph for the end of the lecture "if this is likely to prevent a prompt exit at the sound of the bell.") Each master had to deposit a sum of money in the city bank, from which his fines were deducted.

At French and English universities, where students were younger, masters' guilds had the upper hand. They forbade students to swear or gamble, fined them for breaking curfews and prescribed table manners. "Cleanse not thy teeth," one rule went, "with the steel that is sharpened for those that eat with thee." Students were nevertheless a force to be reckoned with, as they might en masse desert one master's classes for another's. Freshmen —yellowbeaks, as they were called in allusion to young birds—were sometimes advised by upperclassmen to attend several lectures before paying the teacher his fee.

Universities traditionally call up visions of ivied halls and grassy quadrangles. Medieval universities, however, had not even the semblance of permanent quarters. At first lectures were given in wayside sheds at Oxford and Cambridge, in the cathedral cloisters in Paris and in the squares in Italy. In time teachers rented rooms and the students sat on the floor, which was usually covered with straw against the dampness. Unencumbered with buildings, libraries or other equipment, universities could pick up and move elsewhere at any time if they found themselves at odds with local citizens. Cambridge was founded in this way by secession from Oxford.

Secession was not always peaceful. Students grumbled about the high cost of food and lodging, about garbage left in the streets and about the quality of wine in the taverns. Townsmen reciprocated by scorning the airs of both students and masters. Resentment often boiled over into open warfare. Municipal annals of Paris and Oxford contain many accounts of bloody riots in which the opposing factions used swords, pikes, cudgels, bows and arrows, and pails of boiling water and slops hurled from windows. After one Paris riot in 1229, in which several students were killed, masters and students appealed to the Bishop of Paris and the papal legate of Pope Gregory IX. When no help came, they left the town in a body and scattered all over Europe. At length Gregory stepped in, for most students were clerics and therefore under ecclesiastical jurisdiction. He issued a bull granting the university full power to regulate its own affairs, to determine rents and to suspend classes—that is, strike against the town—any time its rights were abrogated. Thereafter the threat of secession was a powerful weapon, for townsmen feared the loss of luster, and of revenue, afforded by a university.

Usually, the university student rose at 4 or 5 o'clock in the morning. After hearing Mass from 5 to 6, he attended classes until 10, when he paused for his first meal of the day—a bit of beef and a thick soup made of its gravy mixed with oatmeal. He then attended classes until 5 in the afternoon, when he went to an almost equally scanty supper. Afterward he went over his notes until 9 or 10. At the day's close at Cambridge, according to one report, "half an hour was devoted to walking or running about, that [the students] might not go to bed with cold feet."

In Italy and the south of France curricula dealt mainly with Roman law or Greek, Arabic and Jewish medicine; in Paris and England with theology, canon law and the liberal arts. Examinations were given at the end of the course of study, which generally took six years. About midway through, the student was questioned orally by his master or by a committee of masters. If he passed, he became a *baccalaureus*, entitled to serve a master as an assistant teacher. Upon completion of his studies he became a master and could teach on his own.

In addition to lectures, the method of teaching was the disputation, in which two or more masters, and occasionally the students, debated text readings, employing Abelard's question-and-answer approach. It was in this context that medieval men developed Scholasticism, a process of painstaking arrival at logical conclusions through questioning, postulating, examining and arranging details into a system of logic. The Scholastic disputation stirred heated clashes and bitter enmities. Wars of logic ran for years between master and master, with adherents of each cheering their hero on with tumultuous stomping and whistling. If it had elements of hootenanny, the disputation was nonetheless the essence of medieval teaching. It trained students to think. It did much to overthrow unquestioning acceptance of the *auctores*. It led to a new ordering of Christianity into a systematic philosophy.

By the 13th Century Christianity was in need of a systematic philosophy. The writings of the ancient Greeks were now pouring into Europe in greater volume, undermining faith and prompting heresies. The whole of Aristotle's *Logic* was now available, and his *Metaphysics* and his works on science had been discovered. Aristotle's doctrines on the nature of the universe were leading men to doubt revelation. From Spain, the works of the

ORIENTAL ARTS

The arts of the Orient during the Middle Ages, created largely for royal patrons, were more social and secular than European works, mainly commissioned by the Church. The illustration above comes from a bestiary—a book depicting the real and imagined beasts of the world—made for the Persian ruler Ghazan Khan at the end of the 13th Century. By then, Persia had already produced two of its finest works of literature: the 11th Century *Book of Kings*, celebrating the Persian past, and the *Rubaiyat*, epigrams in verse by Omar Khayyam. The fabulous tales that became the *Thousand and One Nights* were the literature of the lower classes. Handed down by generations of storytellers, the yarns, derived from folklore, changed with the tellers. They were probably first collected in something resembling their present form in the 15th Century in Egypt.

In China, the Ming Dynasty, beginning in 1368, encouraged a remarkable revival of learning and the arts. In Japan, where the best of medieval literature was written by women, Lady Murasaki's exquisite yet powerful novel, *The Tale of Genji*, was completed about 1010—many centuries before the first novel appeared in Europe.

Moslem philosopher Averroës and the Jewish philosopher Maimonides were spreading skepticism, and most notably at the University of Paris.

The Church could not turn a deaf ear. To quiet the din, Thomas Aquinas was dispatched to Paris from Italy. Thomas was a Dominican monk of noble birth, brilliant mind, tireless industry and gentle disposition. Like Abelard, he honored reason above all other human attributes, but he had distinguished himself for his fidelity to the Church as well as his scholarship. He saw no conflict between faith and knowledge that could not be reconciled by reason. Rather than denounce the tenets of Averroës, Maimonides and Aristotle out of hand, he examined their writings point by point, refuting some and reconciling others with Christianity. The result was his *Summa Theologica* (a summation of theological knowledge), a titanic treatise of 21 volumes dealing with the Christian viewpoint on such matters as logic, metaphysics, theology, psychology, ethics and politics. Accepting Aristotle's principle that every effect has a cause, every cause a prior cause, and so on back to a First Cause, Thomas declared that the existence of God could be proved by tracing all creation back to a divine First Cause, or Prime Mover. Also following Aristotle, he declared that the goal of life is the acquisition of truth.

The mild-mannered Thomas touched off an uproar more acrimonious than the one he was sent to still. First, he was suggesting that knowledge came not solely by divine revelation, but by a deliberate free act of the God-given human mind. He was saying that simple virtue was not enough; man must seek to understand. Second, he had arrived at his conclusions through the logic of Aristotle. Scholars and theologians had for some time now been marveling at the lucidity of Aristotle's reasoning. But few were disposed to have his philosophy incorporated into Christianity. The Bishop

PLATO AND SOCRATES, *cited as authorities on many scholastic issues, appear as prognosticators in this drawing from a 13th Century manuscript which credits Socrates with the power to foretell the sex of a yet-unborn child.*

of Paris branded some of Thomas' propositions as heresy and threatened to excommunicate anyone supporting them. So did two successive Archbishops of Canterbury.

One man rose to counter the charges: Albertus Magnus, a Dominican who had taught Thomas more than 20 years before. At the age of 84 Albertus journeyed from Cologne to Paris, where he entreated the Dominicans to stand by their fellow friar. It took the Dominicans 50 years, but in the end the Church declared that Thomas was a saint and his writings were accepted as completely in accordance with Christian dogma.

Thomism, the philosophy of Thomas Aquinas, now flowed side by side with an older stream of Christian thought. This was the belief propounded eight centuries earlier by St. Augustine, that all necessary knowledge came by divine revelation, not by ratiocination, and that to be pure in heart was more essential to salvation than to be clear of mind. This philosophy was best expressed during the 13th Century by Bonaventura and Duns Scotus. Bonaventura, who was later to become General of the Franciscan Order, taught at the University of Paris while Thomas Aquinas was there. He was well versed in the works of Aristotle but, unlike Thomas, made no attempt to adapt them to the Christian point of view. Bonaventura favored mysticism over reason. Knowledge, he asserted, was less important than love.

Another Franciscan, Duns Scotus, also asserted the primacy of love over intellect. He searched into the power of human intellect and ended by contradicting not only Aristotle, but Thomas as well, saying it was impossible to arrive at a rational knowledge of God.

The rational theory of Thomas and the intuitive theory of Bonaventura and Scotus would coexist in intellectual circles for years to come. In time universities would treat philosophy and theology separately, the first the product of human reason, the second the result of divine revelation.

Literature, too, emerged from the medieval university, although in less solemn fashion. Then as now, students had streaks of ribaldry and nonsense, and scorned their elders. The later medieval era had its show of impudence from the goliards, freeloading footloose scholars who wrote lusty, impious verse glorifying their drinking bouts and escapades with women, parodying the ritual of the Church and lampooning the conventions of the day. The goliards—whose name may have derived from the Latin *gula*, "gullet"—flourished chiefly in Germany and France. But their songs, mostly written in Latin, found their way all through Christendom. Among several that have survived, one goes as follows:

> In the public house to die
> Is my resolution;
> Let wine to my lips be nigh
> At life's dissolution;
> That will make the angels cry,
> With glad elocution,
> 'Grant this toper, God on high,
> Grace and absolution.'

Another variety of medieval versifier was the troubadour, who initially flourished in Provence, in the south of France. The troubadours were pioneer literary exponents of the everyday language of the vernacular as opposed to Latin. Like the goliards, the troubadours were wanderers, and irreverent of the Church. But they idealized gallantry instead of debauchery, and they were not professional scholars, but noblemen and courtiers. The first troubadour was William IX, Duke of Aquitaine, an ex-Crusader and bon vivant who not only dabbled in verse himself but gathered a host of poets around him. His granddaughter, Eleanor of Aquitaine, followed suit. Eleanor was feudal woman at her most flamboyant. When her husband, King Louis VII of France, went off on the Second Crusade in 1147, she fitted herself and her ladies in waiting with breeches and hauberks and set off to join in the fun, trailing an entourage of troubadours behind her. En route, so gossip said, she had affairs with her uncle, Raymond of Poitiers, and with a Saracen slave. Back home again, she secured an ecclesiastical divorce from her royal husband, and married Henry Plantagenet, who two years later became Henry II and made her Queen of England. The troubadours and their art crossed the Channel with her; for all her private peccadilloes, Eleanor's patronage proved a boon to medieval literature.

The troubadours composed their own music and verses and hired minstrels to sing them at court and at tournaments. The earliest lyrics revered woman and celebrated illicit love with pagan abandon. As time went on and feudalism settled into mannered convention, the dalliances of which the knights sang grew more fictitious than real, and their poetry, which began with sensuality in the 12th Century, turned spiritual in the 13th.

In the north of France *trouvères*, less aristocratic and less delicate of manner than the troubadours, were idealizing heroism and adventure in ballads and lays and *chansons de geste*—tales based on history, embellished with fancy and written in verse. All of the *chansons* dealt in some way with Charlemagne, his court and his successors. This genre gave the world one of its greatest epics, the *Song of Roland*, in which Roland, Charlemagne's nephew, lying mortally wounded by the Saracens, refuses to sound his horn to summon Charlemagne's help until he is at the point of death.

After the *chanson* came the *roman*, an ancestor of the modern novel, in which love took a place with war in the affairs of men. The tales of King Arthur and his Round Table, as they accumulated,

IMAGINATIVE CREATIONS *of a 12th Century monk's fertile mind, these exotic people illustrate medieval man's fascinated conjectures about the denizens of distant lands. To the right of the dog-headed man in the top row are three oddities supposedly from India. The fifth man is located, with a distinction not clear today, in the "Orient." Another "Oriental," the first man in the second row, has a lower lip that curls back over his head. The crowned centaur and the horned man with the flutelike nose, in the same row, are "Ethiopians," while the flipper-footed person to the right supposedly comes from "Libya," the ancient Greek name for Africa. Another purported Ethiopian in the bottom row uses his huge foot as a sunshade while a hoofed "Scythian" plays a crude viol. To the right, a giant towers over battling pygmies in India.*

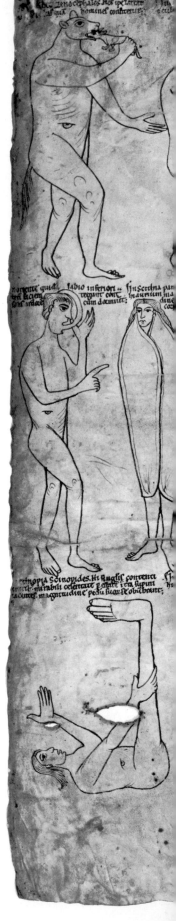

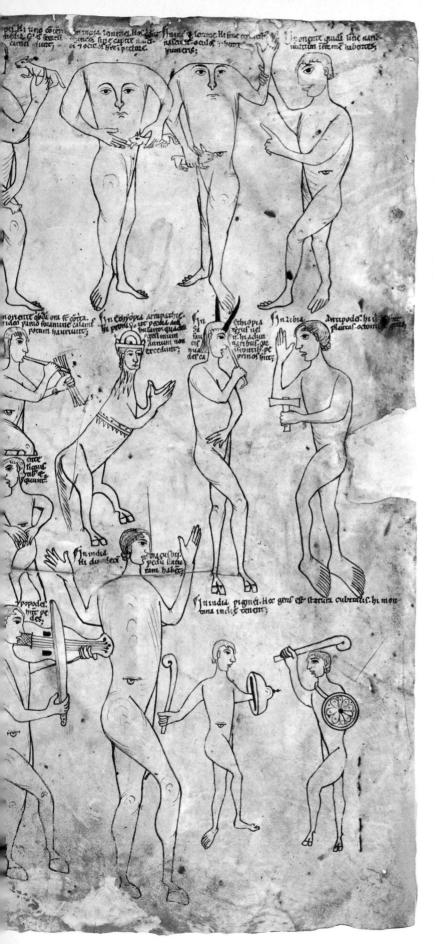

became *romans*. King Arthur was a legendary Sixth Century Briton who defended western England against the Saxons. The account of his prowess was circulated by word of mouth for generations, spreading from Wales through England, France, Germany and down to Italy. By the 12th Century, when the stories of Lancelot's love of Guinevere and the quest for the Holy Grail had been added, Robert of Wace and Chrétien de Troyes, *trouvères* of Jersey and Champagne, put the Arthurian tales into French verse, turning the entire series of narratives into *romans*.

England in this period was still under Norman influence, and French was the language of conversation and letters alike. English did not become established as a language until the 14th Century, with Chaucer's *Canterbury Tales*, a series of stories told by traveling pilgrims in rhymed couplets blending the bawdiness and reverence of the age, and William Langland's *Piers Plowman*, an allegory satirizing the rich, the law and the Church.

German Minnesingers, like the troubadours, moved from court to court and sang of love (*Minne* is archaic German for love). They thrived until the town displaced the manor in importance. In their stead came the Meistersingers, who were products of the artisan and trading classes.

The literature most favored by the bourgeoisie was in the form of *fabliaux*—short metrical tales which satirized feudal conventions, feminine guile, human failings, clerical pomp and Christian ritual. Here was a clear-cut sign of waning respect for authority. By poking barbs at the status quo, satire in any age gives vent to irritation and expresses disenchantment. It pierces such human frailties as sham or avarice and does so in the current idiom; the society it scoffs at is one whose conventions have become stilted and cover a multitude of sins. So it was in 13th Century Europe. Feudalism had become overmannered, courtly love was more affectation than affection, and the clergy cared more for gold than the Golden Rule. The medieval *fabliaux* carried a hint of trouble ahead for the Age of Faith.

At the beginning of the 13th Century, some of the troubadours dispersed to Italy, where they became *trovatori*. The *trovatori* transmitted the northern fashion for ethereal love into the Italian dialects. In less than a century they had molded the language that Dante would call "illustrious, cardinal, courtly, and curial," and that would produce the *Divine Comedy*.

Dante Alighieri was born in 1265 of impoverished Florentine aristocrats. When he was nine he fell in love with Beatrice, a patrician child, who for the rest of his life would haunt his heart and move his pen. At 30 he was elected to the municipal council but was later banished from the city after a coup d'état by the opposition party. Embittered and homeless, he wandered in exile for 19 years, writing now in Latin, now in Italian, of politics, love and philosophy. When at last he created his magnum opus, he called it simply *Commedia* because, he explained, the story passed from despair to happiness and because "it is written in a careless and humble style, in the vulgar tongue, which even housewives speak."

Dante's immortal poem is an account of his passage through hell and purgatory, guided by Vergil, and of his entry into heaven with the spirit of Beatrice. Throughout the journey he discourses on good and evil in the manner of the philosophers. He populates hell and purgatory with nefarious popes and men of state in the manner of the satirists. He makes his love for Beatrice ethereal in the manner of the troubadours. He fits the whole into a complex scheme of mysticism in the manner of the theologians. He describes a foul and murky hell in the superstitious idiom of the folk. Yet throughout, by choosing Vergil to guide him toward salvation, Dante venerates dispassionate wisdom and classic grace in the manner of the Renaissance to come. The *Divine Comedy* is the literary peak of the Middle Ages, for it is at once medieval thought in flower and Renaissance thought aborning.

Two other men, Petrarch and Boccaccio, shared with Dante the founding of Italian letters. At the dawn of the 14th Century, when he wrote, both were adolescents; they would come to maturity with the Renaissance. Petrarch shared Dante's bitterness of temperament but not his penchant for mysticism and allegory; he glorified the sensuous and worldly life. Boccaccio filled his work with good and evil as Dante did, but accepted all sorts and all conditions of men as they were, without Dante's longing for perfection.

The great majority of medieval people comforted themselves, in their short and difficult lives, with hopes of a better life in the world to come. Increasingly, however, there came the humanists, who honored man's temporal aspirations and sought his well-being here and now. With the Renaissance, the humanist point of view would triumph, and its triumph still endures. The emergence of humanism was no accident, but rather a testament to the vision of men like Gerbert and Fulbert, the audacity of men like Abelard and the courage of men like Thomas Aquinas. Dante reaped where all these had sown. Intellectually, he marked the climax of the medieval era.

It was an era that began with the silent scrivening of the monks and culminated in the joyous song of the troubadours. It began with humble obedience to the *auctores*, went on to sober scrutiny of the Faith, and ended with impious mocking of church and state. Superstition and ignorance would linger, but learning at last had passed into the mainstream of society, and thought was venturing farther afield than it had since the Athenian meridian nearly 2,000 years before.

A RESPLENDENT KNIGHT, *the professional soldier of medieval times, is ceremonially armed by his womenfolk with visored helmet and heraldic shield.*

THE FORGING OF A KNIGHT

Sir Geoffrey Luttrell, seen above in a 14th Century illustration, was a product of knighthood in its final form. He was landed, leisured and literate; he followed an elaborate code of chivalry which obligated him to serve, first, his feudal lord, second, the Christian faith and third, a romanticized lady who was not his wife.

Sir Geoffrey was a far cry from the original knights of the Ninth Century. In that turbulent era, kings and lords who were hard pressed by barbarian invaders knighted practically any roughneck who owned a horse. Each knight was granted land in return for military service; each built a crude stronghold on his fief and many rode out plundering. One ruffian, Sir Bevis of Hamton, killed more than 650 people during his depredations. But in the period between Sir Bevis and Sir Geoffrey, while the brutish warriors became courtly aristocrats, knighthood enjoyed its halcyon days and poets preserved its ideals in a timeless literature.

AT BASIC PRACTICE, *two pages fence with toy swords and shields. The would-be knight also sharpened his skills by using lance, sword and battle-ax on the quintain, a post or life-sized dummy.*

ON MARTIAL DUTY, *a squire holds a skittish war horse for his helmeted master. The squire accompanied his knight everywhere but seldom entered combat unless the knight was in mortal danger.*

IN HUMBLE SERVICE, *the squire collects a monk's message for his lord. Youths were taught that chores such as running errands, cleaning armor and waiting on table entailed no loss of dignity.*

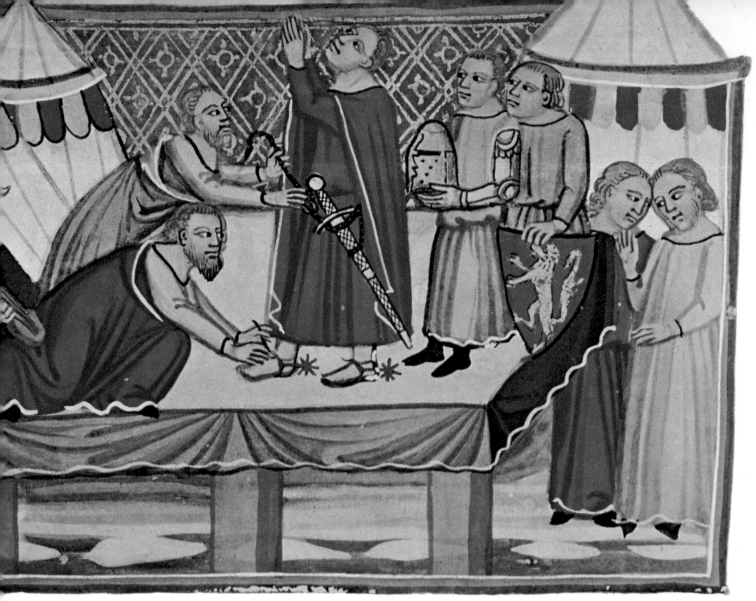

A KNIGHT IS ORDAINED *in a solemn religious ceremony. As he is invested with sword and spurs, musicians strike up a tune on the lute and viol.*

Years of Apprenticeship in the Art of War

To qualify for knighthood, a knight's son would spend about half his life studying the arts of war. At the age of seven the candidate was sent off to serve as a page in a great lord's castle. There he and other pages took lessons in riding and swordsmanship and did various chores. Around the age of 14 he was attached as a squire to an individual knight. Now his training was intensified. To his old chores new duties were added: he dressed his master, cared for the knight's horse and weapons. At about 21 he was dubbed a knight.

In early times, knighthood was conferred on the candidate in a brief, bone-jarring ceremony—the new warrior received a brisk, open-handed blow to his neck, followed by an admonition to conduct himself with bravery, loyalty and skill. But by the 11th Century, the spreading influence of the Church had planted among the knights the seeds of religious chivalry. Soon the act of dubbing grew into a formal rite *(above)* which required of knights a pledge to fight for the Faith and to uphold its moral precepts.

WILY INFIDELS, *approaching a Crusaders' camp in 1270, gain entry by asking to be baptized. Their plot failed, but so did the Crusade.*

SAVAGE CRUSADERS, *battling their way to Jerusalem, use human heads as ammunition for a catapult in besieging Nicaea in 1097.*

DEVOUT KNIGHTS, *led by King Louis IX (wearing crown), set sail for Africa, intent on invading the Holy Land by way of Egypt.*

Soldiers of the Cross in Barbarous Battle

Until November 27, 1095, the knight's obligations to the Faith required little service from him as a professional warrior. But on that day warfare and Christianity were fused by an act of Pope Urban II: he preached a Crusade to free shrines in the Holy Land from the infidels. His sermon launched a series of eight major wars, fought in a 177-year span, in Africa as well as Asia Minor, for the general purpose of suppressing enemies of the Faith. Countless knights eagerly honored their pledge to obey the Church. Great orders of soldier-monks were created, among them the Knights Templars.

All kinds of knights went on crusade—adventurers, freebooters and men as devout as France's King Louis IX *(below)*. Many of them committed terrible atrocities: Crusaders who burst into Jerusalem in 1099 slaughtered thousands. Yet even in the bloodiest campaign some knights were faultless exemplars of their double creed—brave and skillful as warriors, pure and dutiful as men of the Faith.

Fighting for Practice

Even in peacetime, knights rehearsed for war in spectacular tournaments. The joust, a man-to-man contest, is illustrated in the ivory panel above: while two knights are armed by their ladies at right and left, two others meet at a headlong gallop

at center, each with his blunted lance aimed to knock the other out of the saddle. Earlier tests of prowess were less humane. They took the form of the melee, a bloody free-for-all between two bands of knights. In one vast mock battle, fully 3,000 knights tore up acres of vines in the French countryside. Many so-called knights-errant traveled from tourney to tourney; more than one champion amassed a fortune from the armor and ransom that the vanquished had to yield to the victor.

A NIGHT OF FEASTING *begins as attendants carry in food to the lord's family (center) and guests. Each diner here has but one utensil, a knife; all ate with their fingers and tossed bones to the floor for the dogs.*

A GAME OF CHESS *tests the skill—and character—of a noble pair. The game dismayed many a knight unused to long concentration. "The wisest man," noted a contemporary, "loses his patience playing it."*

Lordly Pastimes for Idled Warriors

The 12th Century, with its increasing security and quickening trade, transformed Europe's knights from roving warriors into a settled rural aristocracy, bringing them leisure, hereditary tenure of land and certain amenities of life. Many knights rebuilt their wooden strongholds in stone; these castles slowly grew into elaborate establishments. Here, with their ubiquitous guests and retainers, the knights strenuously feasted, danced and gambled. In quieter moments, they played chess, backgammon and other board games popularized in Europe by returning Crusaders.

But these vigorous, unpolished men seldom stayed indoors in fair weather. They rode, hunted stag and boar, indulged their passion for falconry *(below)*. When no hunt was planned, they worked off their energy at gymnastics and foot races. Sport had replaced warfare as the knights' chief activity.

A PARTY OF HUNTERS *sets out with falcons to catch small game. In the background peasants relax from their labors with a cool dip in the river.*

THE GOD OF LOVE *floats in his heaven at the top of this ivory mirror-back carved in medieval France. He is loosing the darts that cause the mortals below to fall in love.*

For Courtly Knights, Secret Rituals of Romance

The knight was absolute master of his castle—and his wife. Many ladies, resentful of their status, embraced the new concept of courtly love, which was spread by traveling troubadours in the 12th Century. This cult eventually improved the woman's lot by refining her husband's manners—but it also encouraged marital indiscretions by both partners.

Courtly love glorified the relationship of a knight to his chosen lady—which meant any lady but his wife. Its code was as elaborate as the formal gardens in which the lovers often dallied *(left)*. According to formula, the romantic knight must be gay, ardent, secretive and above all courteous. No matter how long the lady withheld her favors, he must continue his courtship undismayed. One dogged knight, Ulrich of Lichtenstein, pursued his lady for 10 years before she granted him an interview.

IN A GARDEN OF LOVE, *knights and ladies exchange amorous banter to the songs of a troubadour. A typical lyric openly proposed, "Lady, take me, body and heart, And keep me for your love."*

The Arthurian Legend: Knighthood Idealized

The supreme expression of romantic chivalry was a body of tales about King Arthur and his Round Table of knights. The real Arthur, it is believed, was a primitive Welsh battle leader of the Sixth Century; but his exploits were embellished by legend until he and his court became the very symbols of medieval knighthood. The Arthurian cycle culminated in the quest for the Holy Grail, the chalice in which Joseph of Arimathea was said to have caught the blood of Christ on the Cross. Arthur's knights are seen at right making vows to search for the Grail. Kneeling at the altar is Sir Galahad, while Arthur, wearing his crown, looks on at left.

In many ways, the quest for the Grail summed up the paradoxes of chivalry and of the knight's historic role. King Arthur, the ideal feudal knight, remained faithful to his duties and stayed at home—yet he was powerless to prevent his kingdom from crumbling. Sir Launcelot was the ideal romantic knight in his love for Arthur's Queen Guinevere—yet because that love was tainted, he was granted only a vision of the Holy Grail. It was the ideal Christian knight, pure and pious Galahad, who actually attained the Grail—and he died without experiencing the illicit delights of courtly love. In fact as in legend, the three sets of knightly ideals were basically incompatible; no knight could ever render perfect service to a feudal lord, the Christian faith and a clandestine ladylove.

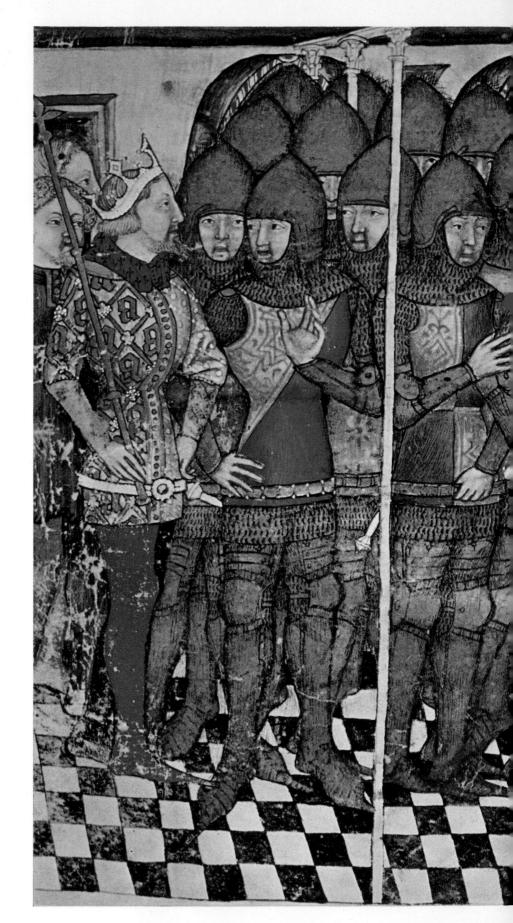

INCIPIT·
LIBER·

6

ART INSPIRED BY FAITH

"Art is the grandchild of God," Dante wrote, and his contemporaries knew well what he meant. Medieval man was convinced of a relationship between the Creation and his own creativity. God had made man; therefore, what man made was only once removed from God and, accordingly, had to be worthy of Him.

In pursuit of this belief, the Age of Faith fashioned its works of superb beauty not "for art's sake," as the Greeks had done, but chiefly for the greater glory of God. The master builder dedicated himself to erecting a house of the Lord. Sculptors, painters, mosaicists, goldsmiths, silversmiths, and inspired craftsmen working in wood, glass and stone dedicated themselves to adorning it. Musicians composed to enhance the rites of worship which the Lord's house sheltered. The skills were diverse, but all art had the same aim: to express in the created the glory of the Creator.

Kneeling before richly carved altars, surrounded by beautiful images bathed in light filtering through stained glass, medieval people felt awed and exalted. It was art's purpose to make them feel so, and thus the art born of faith was as purely functional, in its way, as the art which raises skyscrapers in the service of modern commerce.

Art served another function as well: to attempt to set forth everything that people of the times knew or believed. Victor Hugo noted: "In the Middle Ages men had no great thought that they did not write down in stone."

In the spires, walls, windows, vaults, sculpture, mosaics and murals of the cathedral—the crowning achievement of medieval art—are legible not only man's beliefs and ideals, but also his fantasies and fears, his science, his history—and even his protests: in one bas-relief of Amiens Cathedral, a sculptor who seems to have been irked at feudal arrogance depicted a noblewoman kicking her servant in the stomach.

Medieval art had yet another function, less lofty than the praise of the Lord and the expression of thought. Man, being man, was prideful. Through his creations of art, he tried to prove that he and his neighbors were a little more devout, and therefore a little more worthy of God's gifts, than the folk in the next town. His cathedral's spires had to be the tallest, his cathedral's adornments the most splendid.

The precursors of the great cathedrals began to appear when the Emperor Constantine legalized Christianity throughout the Roman Empire in 313 A.D. and later became a convert himself. Christians could now freely worship outside the catacombs or the seclusion of private homes. To provide a properly imposing architectural setting for the newly sanctioned religion, church-builders adapted the pagan basilica, the spacious rectangular structure with long central aisle, galleries and apse which had served the Romans as marketplace and law court. A few changes adapted the basilica to Christian ritual. Churches were oriented so that the focal point—the altar in the apse—was at the eastern end, the direction of Jerusalem. The entrance was shifted from the middle to the west so that the worshiper, as he came in, faced the altar; its importance as a visual and physical objective was underscored by a rhythmic procession of columns, marching down the central aisle—the nave. Gradually extensions were added on the sides of the nave, giving the ground plan the shape of the Cross and establishing the fundamental form that persists in most Christian churches today.

Although they were externally austere, internally the churches built by Constantine did not lack splendor. Because early Christianity retained the old Hebrew injunction against graven images, its churches had none of the life-sized statues which had adorned pagan basilicas. But light shimmered from precious, polished marble, and glittered from the colored glass-and-gold mosaics which clothed the vast walls. Here again the builders drew upon the past, continuing an art form begun when the Sumerians first fashioned mosaics three thousand years earlier.

Constantine encouraged and financed the construction of dozens of such churches—in North

AN ARCHITECT'S DRAWINGS, *taken from the 13th Century sketchbook of Villard de Honnecourt, reveal geometrical forms within humans, animals and buildings. Below his sketches, Villard wrote: "Here begins the method of drawing as taught by the art of geometry, to facilitate working. And in other sheets will be the methods of masonry." A unique technical manual, the sketchbook is also an architectural document of considerable interest. On his travels as an itinerant "maître d'oeuvre"—a job that combined the functions of architect and master builder—Villard was able to observe at first hand the construction of the great Gothic cathedrals of Rheims and Chartres. With an enthusiasm informed by his experience, he drew what he observed.*

Africa and Asia Minor as well as in Rome, where the style survives in St. Paul Outside the Walls and Sta. Maria in Trastevere.

Two centuries later came the Emperor Justinian, and with him arrived the golden age of Byzantine architecture, with its polygonal buildings. When he succeeded to the Eastern Roman throne in Constantinople in 527, Justinian was both a deeply involved Christian and an unusually active patron of the arts. This combination served to transform, for a time, both the material and spiritual edifices of Christianity.

Building Hagia Sophia ("Divine Wisdom"), the church which remains the unsurpassed exemplar of Byzantine style, Justinian combined a dome with the Roman basilican form. The dome, in the Near East and Orient, had long symbolized divinity. Rising 180 feet above the floor, and ingeniously supported by pendentives or vaultings, this dome seemed virtually to float. The 40 windows and the 40 silver chandeliers which rimmed it served as the central illumination of an interior replete with delicately incised stone carvings, veined marble, and brilliant gold, blue and green mosaics and frescoes.

Ten thousand men toiled for five years—at a cost equivalent to $134 million—to build Hagia Sophia while Justinian, robed in white linen, kerchief on head and staff in hand, urged them on. When it was done, he cried out from its pulpit: "Glory be to God who has thought me worthy to accomplish so great a work! O Solomon! I have vanquished you!"

The grandeur of Justinian's tastes was not to be seen again in Christendom for long centuries. Awash in the barbarian tide, early medieval Europe had all it could do merely to survive. Still, men's esthetic instincts continued to find expression, in activities less monumental than the building of great churches, but no less germinal for the later medieval arts.

The pagan invaders themselves made a notable contribution through their talent for metalworking and woodcarving, applied chiefly in ornaments that were small enough to be carried on their nomadic journeys. The Germanic craftsman favored animal motifs, real or fabled, and intricately interwoven geometric patterns. These designs in time made their way into the stone sculpture and paintings of Romanesque churches, and well before then onto the parchment pages of transcriptions of sacred Christian texts. Distinct traces of the barbarians' "animal style," as art historians have labeled it, appear in two of the extraordinarily rare manuscripts treasured from that era, the Lindisfarne Gospels and the Book of Kells, so called after the Celtic monasteries which produced them, respectively, around 700 and 800.

The scriptoria of the monasteries, intended primarily as workshops where copyists could preserve Christian writings, became centers of artistic enterprise as well. To reproduce the Bible so as to be able to spread the Gospel was not enough. The copies themselves were regarded as objects of veneration whose beauty had to complement the importance of the contents. Monks turned specialists; the *antiquarii* were masters of calligraphy, the *rubricatores* illuminated the initials and the *miniatores* illustrated the margins. Their paintings of Christian themes were not only masterpieces of precision but a triumph over an old bias. "Do not make a picture of Christ," Asterius of Amasia had cautioned in the Third Century, "the humiliation of the Incarnation to which He submitted of His own free will and for our sake was sufficient for Him to endure." Yet by the Sixth Century Pope Gregory the Great had decided that "painting can do for the illiterate what writing does for those who can read," and so the miniaturists worked secure in the knowledge that their endeavors would help propagate the faith.

It was Gregory, too, who gave new impetus to the use of music in the Church. Liturgical chant had always been part of the Christian service. The music, drawn from Greek, Roman and Hebrew sources, was of the simplest monophonic kind, for voices of modest range; yet sung in unison, in a free and flowing rhythm, it had arresting melodic power and expressiveness. Beginning in Gregory's time this *musica plana*—plain song—was reorganized and codified. To insure its uniform adoption, trained teachers were sent out from the Schola Cantorum in Rome. Its acceptance was fervent, although with occasional problems; the Germans, for example, could not handle its soft modulations because, according to one account, their throats were "hoarse from too much drinking." Now known as Gregorian chant, plain song is still the official liturgical music of the Roman Catholic Church today. It also served as a base for the more complex music of later centuries, as inventive monks not only composed melodic variations which they interpolated into the chants but added new harmonizing voices.

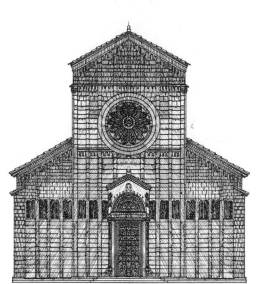

Gregory's dicta on the importance of the arts were unique for his time and for two hundred years thereafter. There was no one of his wide-ranging interests, and of sufficient stature to put them to effect, until Charlemagne. Seeking to enhance the glory of his reconstituted Roman Empire, Charlemagne gave his personal patronage to artistic activity of every sort. The burst of creativity he fostered—called the Carolingian Renaissance —was short-lived but immensely fruitful, fusing for the first time the artistic strains of the Roman, Celtic, Germanic and Byzantine. Much of Carolingian art was small-scale, as in ivory miniatures, illuminated manuscripts, and book covers of gold and enamel studded with jewels. More significant, from a future standpoint, was the resurgence of church-building.

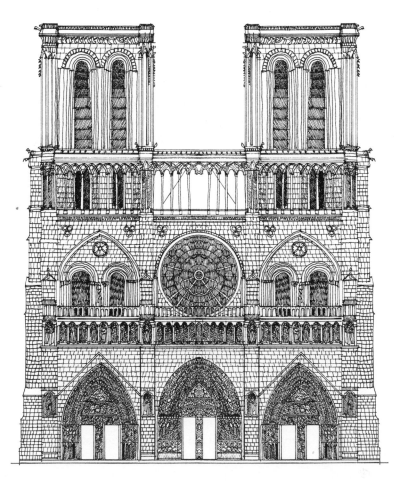

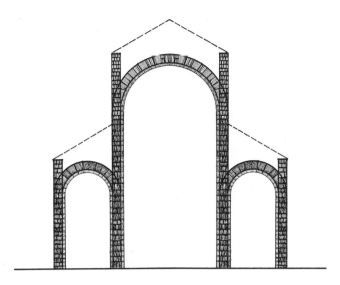

ROMANESQUE AND GOTHIC, *two major styles of architecture that evolved in Europe during the Middle Ages, were, in a sense, variations on the theme of the arched vault. In the 11th and 12th Centuries, church builders, following Roman models, rounded their arches and vaults (above), and built massive walls to carry their weight. By the mid-12th Century, it was found that by pointing the arches, vaults could be built much higher than before. Slender piers, propped by "flying buttresses," supported the soaring Gothic vault (below). With walls freed for windows, churches became virtual skeletons of stone illuminated by magnificent stained glass.*

A distinctive contribution by Carolingian architecture to the great cathedrals of later medieval centuries was to establish the tower as an integral feature of church structures. Churches had had towers as far back as the Sixth Century. They were useful for defense, and also convenient places to hang the bells which summoned the faithful to worship. Under Charlemagne, however, churches acquired multiple towers—bell towers, stair towers, watch towers. Such was the tower's role in the scheme of things that when one feudal lord quarreled with the people of a nearby town, he could think of no worse humiliation for them than to lop off the tower of their church.

Twin towers dominated the royal chapel which Master Odo of Metz, the first Northern architect to be memorialized by name, built for Charlemagne around 800 at his capital at Aachen. Charlemagne probably intended the chapel as his tomb; in any event, it was the most imposing structural achievement Europe had seen for several hundred years. On his visits to Italy, the Frankish monarch had taken note of Constantine's basilicas in Rome and Justinian's Church of San Vitale in Ravenna, finished in 547, a decade after the completion of Hagia Sophia. The Aachen chapel drew on both the Roman and the Byzantine, and added innovations of its own. It had the polygonal shape of the Byzantine, and the massive piers, great round arches, and stately rhythms of the Roman. The symmetrical towers were new. Flanking the entrance, they were so logical a part of it that the entire façade became a single monumental unity. The aim was to impress and overwhelm, and it succeeded superbly. Such entrance structures, called westworks, would become an essential aspect of the cathedrals; the worshiper, approaching, could scarcely help feeling great awe.

Although widespread anarchy marked the later years of the Carolingian dynasty, Charlemagne had ineradicably restored the old tradition of prodigious feats of creativity. To build his chapel had required bold measures, such as the hauling of quantities of stone, columns and bronze gratings across the Alps. The example of obstacles overcome would linger in men's memories, and spur ever more imaginative exploits in the construction of the Romanesque cathedrals which ushered in the golden age of medieval architecture, and of the Gothic cathedrals which marked its climax.

The Romanesque phase began around the mid-11th Century. It was a time of general revitalizing. The popular expectation that the world would end in 1000 A.D.—the millennium of the Apocalypse—had gone happily unfulfilled. The Church was in the process of reforming recent evils. Imbued with a renewed sense of faith, ordinary folk began to undertake lengthy pilgrimages to Christendom's great shrines. Places were required where they could pause and worship en route. The result manifested itself in a *morbus aedificandi*, as contemporary chronicles called it, a disease of building; it has been estimated that 1,587 churches were built in France alone during the 11th Century. The Cluniac monk Raoul Glaber wrote that "it was as though the very world had shaken herself and cast off her old age, and were clothing herself everywhere in a white garment of churches."

Under this stimulus, the Romanesque style developed and matured. Ultimately it evolved multiple variations—among others, Tuscan, Sicilian, Rhenish and Norman—but all had the same basic characteristics. At first, materials were of brick or small stone, because the builders had not yet learned to handle heavier stone. Because wooden roofs frequently burned, the Romanesque church was topped by a thick half cylinder of stone, a barrel vault—whose very weight, however, could spread the walls and send them toppling. To compensate, walls were thickened at points of stress, and piers were made massive. Windows were few and small. Arches were round, as in the Roman style from which the Romanesque took its name.

What the Romanesque interior lacked in light it made up in gleaming color. Walls were hung with tapestries and painted bright green, blue or violet; similar hues covered vaultings and columns. Chandeliers gave off a golden glow. Effigies of saints were gilded. Illuminated books used in the services were bound in carved ivory or gold inlaid with jewels. Reliquaries were studded with immense gems. Chalices were elaborately ornamented with enamel, or set with rubies, emeralds, sapphires and pearls.

Sculpture, too, was employed to lighten the heavy Romanesque effect. Having long lain fallow, the stonecarver's art blossomed with an exuberance that sometimes seemed to covet every surface in sight. No heed was paid to classical proportions; shapes were bent, twisted, stretched or reduced to fit a specific space. Like the miniaturists of the manuscript workrooms, the Romanesque sculptor felt that his mission was to educate as well as decorate. On the capitals of columns inside the church, and outside on the portals and the tympanums over the doors, he displayed a dazzling virtuosity of subject matter. While religious themes predominated, they were by no means all. Around 1125 the powerful Abbot Bernard of Clairvaux was driven to complain: "To what purpose are those unclean apes, those fierce lions, those monstrous centaurs, those half-men, those striped tigers, those fighting knights, those hunters winding their horns? . . . In short, so many and so marvellous are the varieties of divers shapes on every hand, that we are more tempted to read in the marble than in our books, and to spend the whole day in wondering at these things rather than in meditating the law of God. For God's sake, if men are not ashamed of these follies, why at least do they not shrink from the expense?"

Among the greatest Romanesque churches were those attached to the monasteries. During this period, the monastic orders commanded resources far exceeding those of the bishops in the towns; they also had a plentiful supply of peasant labor. Though the builders and their helpers learned by trial and error, engineering knowledge was limited. Romanesque remained ponderous and earthbound. Gothic architecture banished this inhibition, solving problems which its predecessor had never quite managed to overcome.

The features most closely identified with the Gothic style—the pointed arch, the ribbed vault, the buttress—were not, in strict fact, its original creations. Here and there the adventurous Romanesque builder had experimented with them. Because, by sheer mathematical dictate, the height of the curve of the round arch was limited to half the width of its base, he had tried to achieve greater height by the pointed arch, which could be raised to any level commensurate with its tensile strength. He had used stone ribs to form the vaultings, and buttressed the walls with masses of outside masonry, to counter the downward and outward thrust of the vaults and heavy roof. The triumph of the Gothic builder was to improve these features, refine them, and, above all, fuse them into a totally harmonious working partnership.

The ribbed vault and the pointed arch became parts of the same continuous whole. The support provided by the outside masonry was reinforced; now projected from it were stone bridges which arched through the air—hence, flying buttresses—and were connected to the church at the points where the roof and vaulting pressed most insistently on the nave walls. As the Gothic builder became more exquisitely precise in his calculation of stresses and strains and thrusts and counterthrusts, the massive piers of the Romanesque interior were replaced by clusters of colonnettes, thick walls

yielded to tremendous windows, and vaults and spires soared ever higher. Where the Romanesque had been solid, closed-in, brooding, the Gothic was graceful, uninterruptedly spacious, wondrously filled with light. Not until the 20th Century skyscraper would architecture achieve so stunning a feat. Ironically, the Gothic acquired its name as a term of derision calling up the memory of the barbarian Goths; the epithet was devised by men of the Renaissance who disdained the Gothic builders' failure to adhere to the classic standards of Greece and Rome.

As a distinctive style, the Gothic first appeared in the restoration of the abbey church of St.-Denis, near Paris. The reconstruction was begun in 1137; in 1144 fourteen bishops and five archbishops consecrated the altars, and King Louis VII with 12 knights played the part of Christ and the Apostles. The occasion was a time of special elation for the Abbot of St.-Denis, Suger, who had conceived and guided the work of rebuilding. Suger was a man of humble birth and brilliant intellect who had risen high not only in the Church but in royal esteem. The old abbey over which he presided had been the site of the consecration of both Charlemagne and his father, Pepin the Short, and the burial place of Pepin and his father, Charles Martel. Mindful of these associations with the first great leaders of the Franks, Suger perceived that an impressive church edifice could serve a purpose beyond the spiritual—that it could kindle the national spirit of his countrymen as well.

Pursuing this vision, Suger spared no effort. He personally sought out the timber for the beams. He summoned the best builders, artists and workmen Europe could provide and invited the free play of their ideas, although his own predominated. He also kept a running account of progress so meticulous in its detail that it remains a treasured source on Gothic architecture. He noted, for example, the time a terrible storm arose while "the main arches —standing by themselves—were not yet held together . . . by the bulk of the vaults . . . a force of contrary gales hurled itself against the aforesaid arches, not supported by any scaffolding nor resting on any props." The new ribbed, pointed arches withstood this tremendous buffeting—a phenomenon attributed by Suger not to their tensile strength but to the timely intercession of God and the saints.

Suger described his reaction to the work of restoration in terms seldom improved upon in later literary paeans to the Gothic: "I seemed to find myself, as it were, in some strange part of the universe which was neither wholly of the baseness of the earth, nor wholly of the serenity of heaven, but by the grace of God I seemed lifted in a mystic manner from this lower towards that upper sphere."

Shortly after the new Church of St.-Denis had shown the way, work began on cathedrals at Sens, Senlis and Noyon, and in 1163 on Notre-Dame in Paris. Bishops and towns everywhere competed to produce the grandest, tallest edifices. They were frankly out to break records. Siena looked at the Duomo of Florence and decided to convert its own church into a mere transept for a cathedral. Notre-Dame in Paris raised a vault to 114 feet. Chartres, begun in 1194, surpassed it with 123 feet, only to be surpassed in turn by Rheims with 124 feet, and Amiens with 138 feet. Beauvais, jealous of Amiens, aimed 19 feet higher, but the vault collapsed; undaunted, Beauvais rebuilt it, only to have it collapse again in 1284. Still undaunted, Beauvais tried again, aiming for 157 feet. But Beauvais ran out of money, as many towns did, and left the church without transept or nave.

The construction of the cathedrals was financed by a variety of methods. One was the sale of indulgences by the Church; Rouen's south tower is called the Butter Tower because it was built with

GREGORIAN MUSIC *is unaccompanied vocal melody. On the 14th Century missal page, above, the line representing C is indicated at the beginning of each four-line staff by a primitive clef sign—two notelike marks flanking the line. Elsewhere, where one note is written above another, the bottom note is sung first. For comparison, the last four lines of the left-hand column of the missal are transcribed in modern style below. Although musical notation has since changed—notes now have time values; the staff has five lines —the music itself has not. It is still chanted in Catholic and Episcopal churches. The Latin text of the transcribed lines reads: "The Lord be with you. And with thy spirit. Lift up your hearts. We lift them up unto the Lord."*

money from dispensations sold to permit the eating of butter during Lent. Relics were paraded in processions throughout the country, and people gave contributions for the privilege of venerating them, the money going to the local cathedral's building fund. Kings bestowed annuities, noblewomen their jewels. Priests asked parishioners for contributions.

People gave not only money, but labor. Archbishop Hugo of Rouen described the mood of the times in a letter to Bishop Thierry of Amiens: "The inhabitants of Chartres have combined to aid in the construction of their church by transporting the materials . . . the faithful of our diocese and of other neighbouring regions have formed associations for the same object; they admit no one into their company unless he has been to confession, has renounced enmities and revenges, and has reconciled himself with his enemies. That done, they elect a chief, under whose direction they conduct their waggons in silence and with humility."

The building of a cathedral took sometimes one, usually several generations; Notre-Dame in Paris was not completed until around 1250, nearly 90 years after its start. Many cathedrals were never finished. But while work was in progress, towns poured all of their energies into the projects. The Gothic cathedral was as much a creation of the town, and of the busy crafts which town life had fostered, as the Romanesque had been a creation of the rural community and the quiet skills of monks and peasant helpers.

A cathedral site resembled a huge construction camp, with its jumble of windlasses, hand winches, treadwheels and other leverage machines, and, everywhere, cartloads of stone brought from nearby quarries in endless procession. The work on the cathedral was contracted to a group of craftsmen working cooperatively—masons, carpenters, stonecutters, sculptors, workers in metal and stained glass. Some might remain together as a team for years, sometimes moving on in a body to another cathedral project when one had been completed. Usually directing the group were two men: an architect who supervised the entire endeavor, and a manager who secured the materials and labor. Uprooted serfs and peasants provided the pool of common laborers—the men who quarried stone, transported timber, dug the cathedral foundations, and carried the slate for its roof and other materials in baskets on their backs.

Of the crafts involved, the masons were specially privileged. They were favored with such niceties as gloves to protect their hands against lime burns, and were given a gratuity when the keystone of the cathedral was set in place. The architects, the professional elite, enjoyed even greater emoluments, including exemption from taxation, free housing, robes of fur and a year-end bonus.

The requirements of cathedral-building inspired ingenuity at every level of craftsmanship. The jewel-like colors of the translucent stained-glass windows, shedding a brilliant glow on the gray stone of cathedral interiors, have never been duplicated. The massive cathedral roofs were so fashioned that a single defective piece could be removed and replaced. To keep both roofs and walls free of rain water, spouts were set along the cornices; not content with making them merely utilitarian, cathedral workers turned them into fanciful birds or beasts of stone—gargoyles, or little "throats"—that spewed jets of water a safe distance from the building. Blacksmiths devised stronger steel tools for cutting stone to precise measure, iron straps for lifting great weights, iron chains for reinforcing the masonry from within. Carpenters devised ramps to pull wagonloads of materials up steep ascents and even hit upon that astonishing apparatus, the wheelbarrow, which enabled one man to accomplish the work of two.

A marvel of ethereal beauty, filled with glorious

light, color and music, adorned with tapestries, paintings and sculpture, the Gothic cathedral was everything to medieval man—his house of worship, his school, library, art gallery, theater. The cathedral was the very heart of town life. On the steps, or in the public square outside it, mystery and miracle plays were performed, and civic affairs were threshed out in crowded assemblies. Near it markets and fairs drew throngs. Sometimes commercial and social activity expanded into the building itself. At Chartres, merchants set up stalls within its precincts, strangers slept under its portals, and citizens—some with their dogs or falcons—promenaded in the side aisles, exchanging small talk. The cathedral was not only a house of the Lord but also a house of the people.

Along with the flowering of medieval architecture came a flowering of the other major arts. Improved musical notation helped both the performance and the preservation of music. Moving away from the monophonic chant, composers such as Guillaume de Machaut of France and Francesco Landini of Italy developed a passion for polyphony, in which two or more distinct melodies were united. In the 14th Century "choral chapels" which specialized in this music began to employ choruses of 12 to 24 voices to sing the new works which would influence such giants as Bach, Haydn, Beethoven and Brahms. Madrigals, rounds and motets became the fashion. Folk songs spread far and wide. Not all were religious in theme; many celebrated daily life and work, love and beauty, heroism and the hunt.

Sculpture, which was formerly incorporated in columns and portals, took on more three-dimensional realism, seeming to stand free. Distorted forms gave way to figures of recognizable proportions, represented with symmetry and clarity. Rigid and mask-like facial expressions were supplanted by the human and gentle. The renowned *Beau Dieu*, on the west façade of the Cathedral at Amiens, depict-ed Christ in classic draperies, carrying the Book of the Gospels in His left hand, His right hand raised in benediction—a ruler altogether benevolent and just. The naturalism of Renaissance sculpture was aborning.

Painting, long the preserve of miniaturists in the scriptoria and of fresco artists in the churches, moved into urban workshops. The miniaturists were no longer solely concerned with didactic illustrations of sacred manuscripts. They now had secular patrons, for whom they produced private prayer books in which pages were devoted to vividly detailed paintings of medieval life and landscapes. Fresco and panel painters began a search for new techniques. In Italy, Giotto broke ground for the use of perspective, and raised questions about the treatment of human anatomy which set off an intensive period of experimentation by his followers. Among them, Masaccio, painting his frescoes in the Brancacci Chapel in Florence, depicted the naked human form, male and female, with a stark power and vitality that would inspire both Leonardo and Michelangelo. In Flanders, the brothers Hubert and Jan Van Eyck used oil as a medium to achieve new effects of color and texture.

The arts were becoming increasingly secular, and Gothic architecture itself was losing much of its precise workmanship. Later Gothic edifices were no longer harmonious elevations of stone and glass, reaching up to heaven to seek and receive the light. Cathedrals became overdecorated and overornamented. They were cluttered with cherubic faces and stalactites of lace, and pinnacled, turreted and embroidered with galleries and gables—a riot of excess and excrescence.

But the glory of Gothic at its best remained. Those who had built its great exemplars had built them to last, and they survive, splendid still, in Europe today, a testament to man's capacity to infuse his artistic achievements with his faith.

IN GOTHIC MAJESTY, *the Cathedral—silvery gray and infinitely graceful—rises high above Chartres.*

QUEEN OF CATHEDRALS

Between 1170 and 1270, more than 500 great French churches were built in the Gothic style. One of the greatest rose on a wheat-rich prairie 54 miles southwest of Paris, in a town whose citizens had long believed that the Virgin Mary preferred their church to any other as her residence on earth. Resolving to erect a new cathedral truly worthy of heaven's queen, the 10,000 townspeople poured all of their energies and resources into the project, and an army of anonymous craftsmen brought to bear all of the arts and technical skills of the age. The final product, Notre-Dame of Chartres, stands today as the epitome of Gothic grandeur—faith translated into a soaring monument of carved stone and stained glass.

CHARTRES' WEST PORTAL *constitutes a veritable "Bible in stone." The 19 tall statues that flank its three doors represent Old Testament figures. The*

Faith and Works

The oldest part of the Cathedral's superstructure is the west façade, whose magnificent portal *(above)* dates back to 1145. The statuary framing the doors exemplifies that period's transitional art, combining the stylized severity of the Romanesque with the warmer, freer naturalism of the Gothic.

The west portal was built to beautify the 11th Century church that stood behind it. But on June 10, 1194, disaster struck Chartres. A great fire destroyed the church—except for its new façade. The

tympanum above the central door portrays Christ in majesty, while the other tympanums illustrate Christ's Incarnation (right) and His Ascension.

stunned citizens feared that the flames had consumed their most precious relic—the tunic which the Virgin Mary was said to have worn at Christ's birth. But miraculously the relic survived.

In pious gratitude, the townspeople gave huge sums to rebuild the Virgin's church in matchless splendor. The Bishop of Chartres, whose diocese was one of the largest in France, and who received from it an annual income equal to some $1.5 million, committed most of this fortune to construc-

tion. Additional funds were raised at local fairs, and by exhibiting Chartres' relics on foreign tours.

The townspeople contributed their labor as well as their money. Joined by devout volunteers of every class and from every region, they harnessed themselves to carts and dragged huge blocks of stone from the quarry, seven miles distant.

The new Notre-Dame, incorporating the superb west façade, emerged from the rubble of the old and climbed slowly above the rooftops of Chartres.

Animated Carvings for Lavish New Portals

As Notre-Dame grew, it mirrored the humanizing trend of the times. By 1215 the builders had raised the main body of the Cathedral, and work was in progress on the transept—the lateral wings that gave the church its cruciform shape. Chartres' transept, the largest in France, was dressed with two sumptuous portals. The sculptures ordered for both portals took on a new animation and individuality.

These qualities, hallmarks of the mature Gothic style, pervade the statues at right, which guard the middle door of the south portal. Mounted on the center post is a grave but vital figure of Christ as teacher. At right are realistic statues of St. Paul, St. John and St. James the Great. The relief above Christ's head, part of the Last Judgment, shows St. Michael *(foreground)* separating the elect *(left)* from the damned *(right).* This stately treatment of the theme conveys a sense of resignation rather than the anguish and desperation of Romanesque versions. Through the open doorway can be seen dazzling examples of another Gothic triumph—the vivid stained-glass windows above Chartres' north portal.

Charlemagne and his peers, from the Window of Charlemagne.

The Creation of Eve, from the Good Samaritan Window.

The Death of the Virgin, from the Window of the Assumption.

Mary nursing the Infant Jesus.

An angel from one of Chartres' few restored panels.

The Crucifixion and the Deposition from the Cross.

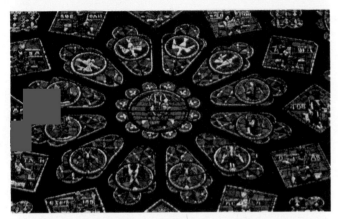

Christ enthroned in majesty, from the Window of the Tree of Jesse.

"The Rose of France": the Glorification of the Virgin.

St. Nicholas, from a window depicting legends of his life.

Creating Walls of Multihued Glass

The art of making stained glass, given new impetus by the Gothic style in the 1140s, was raised to its zenith a half century later by craftsmen at Chartres. The glassmakers' basic formula called for sand, salt and ashes. Stained glass was made by heating this mixture into a molten mass, then coloring it with metallic oxides—copper for red, iron for yellow, cobalt for blue. Thin fragments of colored glass were worked into the grooves of malleable lead frames, forming panels. Only after all the panels had been mounted in the window could the glaziers judge the brilliance of their colors and the impact of their design.

Time has been kind to their 12th and 13th Century handiwork: Chartres still possesses most of its original glass—and many of the greatest windows ever created. Some of the 176 windows were paid for by noblemen and prelates. The nation's royal house donated a great rose window 33 feet in diameter—the "Rose of France" *(left)*. But many windows were given by Chartres' merchants and craftsmen: furriers (the Charlemagne Window), shoemakers (the Good Samaritan Window), bakers and even water-carriers. Their symbols in the windows attest eloquently to the democracy of faith.

Glorifying the Virgin in a Treasury of Art

Notre-Dame was not only named after the Virgin; sculptors and glassmakers exalted her in many ways throughout the church. They depicted Mary on a larger scale than custom dictated. They portrayed her as mother of Christ, Queen of Heaven, intercessor for sinners and the symbol of the Church. One of Chartres' finest windows, shown in part at right, clothes Mary in a double radiance: she holds her son Jesus and she wears her celestial crown.

Great prominence was given to the legends of Mary's early life and her many relatives. St. Simon, one of her six nephews, was portrayed in a major statue. In the photograph opposite, he stands at left, in the august company of St. Matthew *(center)* and St. Paul *(lower right)*.

When the artists had finished, Chartres boasted the most comprehensive decoration of any church. Its windows and statuary present nearly 10,000 figures enacting the whole story of God and man from the creation of the universe to the end of time. In this immense pageant, Mary ranks second only to Christ in importance, and the entire Cathedral asserts her glory.

Consecrating "This Place of Awe"

In 1260, the great Cathedral was finally consecrated. Thousands came to attend the ceremony: townspeople of Chartres, peasants from outlying villages, prelates and visiting lords. The huge throng was easily accommodated in the cavernous church, seen here in an unusual photograph that reveals its full 427-foot length, from the apse (*bottom*), down the nave, to the rose window high in the west façade (*top*). Along both sides of the nave, graceful piers soar upward and flare out into the cross-ribbed vault 123 feet above the floor; and between these supports, the upper walls of the Cathedral dissolve into floating bursts of stained-glass color. The total effect is so overwhelming that the worshipers in 1260 must have accepted literally the words intoned in the Mass for the consecration of a church: "This is a place of awe. Here is the court of God and the gate of Heaven."

THE LOFTY CATHEDRAL, *seen from the south of Chartres, dominates the fields whose rich harvests helped to finance its construction. Summing*

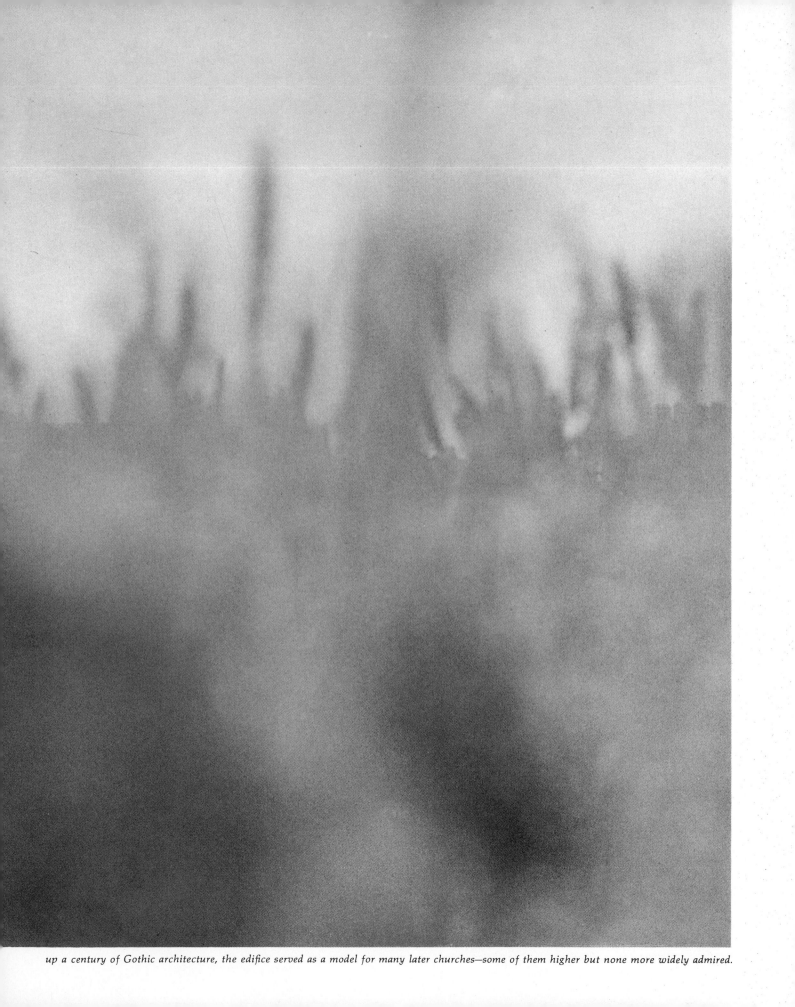

up a century of Gothic architecture, the edifice served as a model for many later churches—some of them higher but none more widely admired.

7

THE NATION-STATES

Politically, Europe at the close of the 11th Century was a hodgepodge. From Sicily in the south to England in the north, the reins of authority lay variously in the hands of kings, lords, barons, dukes, counts, bishops and princes. Land was the mark of their wealth and the source of their power. A king was not especially important; his position varied according to his own strength or weakness. He was only a lord among lords; some were his vassals, and some were independent. A king might have less land and fewer vassals than the lords whose territories surrounded his.

But Europe was beginning to outgrow the feudal system, which had arisen in a sequestered, agrarian way of life. Feudalism had no answers to the social and economic problems created by the growth of towns, the expansion of trade, the use of money and the birth of technology. The relations of men to their fellows were shifting, and the old institutions of feudalism no longer sufficed to maintain the social order. New ways had to be devised to manage human affairs. The men who saw these facts of social life and understood the uses of power laid the groundwork, in the 12th and 13th Centuries, for the modern nation-state.

The state was a new entity, with defined geographical boundaries, which kept order within and repelled invasion from without. It centralized functions that under feudalism had been diverse and irregular. It came to oversee a widening range of human concerns: the administration of justice, the securing of rights, in some places the regulation of industry and in some the regulation of health and medicine. The state rested on written legislation; it allowed participation by more and more members of society; it functioned by means of a corps of civil servants who administered in its name throughout the realm; and it financed itself by the levy of taxes.

The state was built by the monarchy, which in its existing form had evolved out of feudalism. The leading states were France and England, which in their separate ways cast the molds of administration and justice that would eventually be followed in countries all over Europe. Italy and Germany resisted centralized monarchy until long after the Middle Ages were past, but in those regions, too, written legislation replaced word-of-mouth tradi-

EUROPE IN THE 1360s *was a continent in transition. Much of Eu-rope was still divided into feudal holdings in which patriotism was still provincial. However, the nation-states of England and France had taken more solid form. To the south, the frequently quarreling Christian kingdoms of the Iberian peninsula had united at times to fight the Moslems, who still occupied Granada.*

The Holy Roman Empire, dominated by magnates who were often at odds with one another, was a unity in name only. Italy, par-celed out among the Holy Roman Empire, the papacy, and foreign dynasties ruling in Naples and Sicily, was centuries from unifica-tion. In southeast Europe, the weak Byzantine, Serbian and Bul-garian states were easy prey to Turkish advances from the east.

EUROPE IN TRANSITION

N

FAEROES

SHETLAND
ISLANDS

ORKNEY
ISLANDS

Bergen

NORWAY

SWEDEN

Oslo

Stockholm

ESTONIA

BALTIC

SEA

Riga

TEUTONIC KNIGHTS

SCOTLAND

Edinburgh

NORTH
SEA

DENMARK

Copenhagen

PRUSSIA

Danzig

Vilnius

IRELAND

Dublin

Cork

ENGLAND

London

LITHUANIA

Vistula R.

POLAND

Kiev

Dni

ATLANTIC

OCEAN

ENGLISH CHANNEL

Calais

PONTHIEU

Cologne

Rhine R.

HOLY
ROMAN
EMPIRE

Elbe R.

SILESIA

Bremen

Paris

PALATINATE

BOHEMIA

Prague

Kraków

FRANCE

Ratisbon

BAVARIA

Vienna

Danube R.

BAY OF
BISCAY

SWISS
CONFED

AUSTRIA

Buda Pest

MOLDAVIA

HUNGARY

Bordeaux

Limoges

AQUITAINE

León

Rhone R.

Venice

WALACHIA

Avignon

PROVENCE

Genoa

VENICE

Bucharest

NAVARRE

Marseilles

Florence

Nicopolis

PORTUGAL

CASTILE

ARAGON

CORSICA

PAPAL
STATES

Rome

ADRIATIC

SEA

SERBIAN

BULGARIA

Sofia

Lisbon

Toledo

PRINCIPALITIES

BYZANTINE

Granada
GRANADA

BALEARIC ISLANDS

SARDINIA

NAPLES

Durazzo

Thessalonica

EMPIRE

MEDITERRANEAN SEA

Palermo

Messina

AEGEAN
SEA

SICILY

KNIGHTS OF
RHODES

MOSLEM STATES

CRETE

tion in meting out justice and keeping order, and human rights were recognized.

The modern English monarchy was founded by William, Duke of Normandy, who conquered the Anglo-Saxons in 1066. He began by demanding an oath of fealty from every Anglo-Saxon lord, confiscating the property of any who refused. Rather than bestow large holdings that might be seedbeds of opposition, he gave small and scattered fiefs to the Norman knights who had crossed the Channel with him. He established a *Curia regis*, or king's council, in which he placed his vassals and high churchmen, and summoned it to do his bidding, keep his accounts and try disputes that concerned the Crown.

William made the existing shires (counties) fiscal and military units of the realm, but he allowed their courts of justice to operate autonomously under local lords, as in Anglo-Saxon times. To ascertain exactly how much property he had and how much was his due, he sent commissioners out to all the counties to assess the land and determine the number of freemen and villeins, meadows and farms, oxen and pigs, plowshares and mills. The survey was completed in 1086, and the results were recorded in the *Domesday Book*, which can still be seen in the Public Record Office in London.

By the time of his death in 1087, William had made the English monarchy the most advanced in Europe. The lords were his vassals and gave him direct allegiance. The *Curia regis* served his will and helped keep peace among the lords. The *Domesday Book* gave him a thorough inventory of his assets and a basis for taxation.

Under the reign of his youngest son, Henry I, the *Curia regis* developed two separate and specialized functions: one judicial, the other financial. Henry sent members of the *Curia* out across the land to try disputes where they arose instead of bringing them before the King's court. These men were the precursors of the circuit judges in England and the United States today. The financial part of the *Curia* developed almost by default. Many of the barons were bored or baffled by record-keeping and arithmetic, and so they stayed away when there was reckoning to be done. Those who attended grew into a competent group of accountants. They did their tallying on a checkered tablecloth, and from this came the name of the Exchequer, the royal treasury. The qualification for serving in the *Curia* ceased to be nobility and came to be expertise. Henry took to paying some of his men in coin instead of with parcels of land, and thus he developed a corps of professional civil servants.

The next step toward making England a modern state was the writing of constitutional law, and this came with Henry II, a great-grandson of William the Conqueror. Henry was more French than English. He had, in fact, more lands on the Continent than the French King. Through his father he was Count of Anjou and of Maine. Through his marriage to Eleanor of Aquitaine he acquired Poitou, Guienne and Gascony. He had had several years' experience in government as reigning Duke of Normandy when in 1154, at the age of 21, he ascended the English throne.

Henry's major aim was to wipe out feudal warring once and for all, and one means to this end was to improve the courts of justice.

The Anglo-Saxons, like most Germanic peoples, had tried civil disputes and breaches of custom by calling the accused before the elders of the tribe. Their usual methods of trial were compurgation, wager of battle, and ordeal. In compurgation, friends of the accused would swear to his good character and thus, by implication, to his innocence. In wager of battle, two antagonists would go at each other with fists or clubs. In both cases God was expected to intervene—to strike dead the man who lied and to cause the virtuous man to win the fight. In trial

Map labels:
•Moscow

RUSSIAN STATES

KHANATE OF THE GOLDEN HORDE

BLACK SEA

TURKISH STATES

CYPRUS

by ordeal, the accused might be tossed into a pool of water. If he sank, he was deemed innocent (and was presumably fished out). If he floated, he was declared guilty and fined or put to death. In Henry's time these customs still prevailed all over Europe.

Henry altered the settling of civil disputes by introducing the practice of inquest, or investigation. He had the royal circuit judges call in neighbors of the litigants, usually 12, and question them about the case in dispute. When the answers of all 12 neighbors agreed, the result was said to be *vere dictum*, the Latin for truly spoken; hence the English "verdict." The earliest verdicts may have been tainted by gossip or otherwise faulty, but they nevertheless marked a significant step toward securing justice. They loosed the medieval mind from superstition, and before long judges were not only consulting jurors but seeking evidence for the answers they gave. Henry permitted the privilege of inquest to any freeman in certain instances, and because he reserved to himself the right to authorize it, the barons lost much of their local judicial power. The lesser gentry liked the system at once, and Henry soon extended it to criminal cases as well.

He next dealt with the discrepancies between secular and ecclesiastical rights. Clerics—and this meant not only priests and monks, but all Crusaders, all students, and all servants of churchmen; hence a large segment of the population—were by tradition immune from civil trial. Many a cleric went free of punishment for an offense that would have brought fine, imprisonment or death to a lay citizen. Henry sought to end the abuse of clerical privileges. In 1164 he gathered his councilors at the royal estate in Clarendon Park, not far from Salisbury, and there in a hunting lodge they drafted what came to be known as the Constitutions of Clarendon. The document declared clerics bound by the customs of the realm. It prohibited appeals to the Pope over royal decisions, forbade excom-

munication of royal vassals and government officials without the knowledge of the king, and decreed that a criminal cleric convicted in an ecclesiastical court must be turned over to a royal court for punishment.

The Constitutions of Clarendon marked a milestone in legal history but had unfortunate consequences. Henry had an old friend and comrade in Thomas à Becket, who had been appointed Archbishop of Canterbury at Henry's behest. Becket, a man of worldly tastes turned righteous in episcopal office, first accepted and then refused to honor the Constitutions of Clarendon and excommunicated the bishops who supported the King. The issue simmered for several years and at last Henry was seized with anger. "Is there no one to rid me of this miserable clerk?" he cried. A band of knights thereupon took the King at his word, ambushed Becket in his cathedral and murdered him. Henry ruefully said he had not meant violence, but the incident proved a setback for the Crown. The barons were becoming restive under Henry's growing power, and the murder of Becket gave them an excuse to fight back.

The next stride toward constitutional government, therefore, was taken not by a reforming king, but by conservative noblemen seeking to halt the advance of the monarchy. Henry's son John—nicknamed "Lackland" and "Softsword" by his subjects—was one of the most erratic and unscrupulous kings England has ever had. He was long on grandiose ideas, for which he taxed heavily, but short on the perseverance needed to carry them out. The extensive English holdings in France had dwindled to a narrow strip along the Atlantic. Philip II had confiscated all but Poitou and Guienne. John set off to recover the French territories, but after his troops had suffered a crushing defeat at the Battle of Bouvines in 1214, he went home to find the barons and clergy irate.

A FAMILY TREE, *from the 12th Century Decree of Gratian, depicts in cruciform the great range of blood-connected relations within a given family. At the top, below the head of Adam, are the great-great-great-grandparents. At center, mother and father appear twice, as children and as parents. An important document in medieval canon law, Gratian's table of consanguinity was mainly consulted to prevent marriage between closely related kin.*

Stephen Langton, Archbishop of Canterbury, exhorted the barons to demand the rights they had exercised under Henry I a hundred years before. One by one they renounced their allegiance to the King. Secret meetings were held, rebellion was plotted, statements of rights were drafted and drafted again. Finally, after months of mounting tension, a small band of lords and their knights armed themselves and marched on the King. In June of 1215 they confronted him at Runnymede, a meadow on the banks of the Thames, 20 miles outside of London. There they wrangled for days until John finally gave in and put his seal to Magna Carta, one of the great landmarks of Western civilization.

Magna Carta was written in Latin on a parchment scroll. Many copies were made and sent to cathedrals all over England for safekeeping. The sheriffs were required to read it aloud in the county courts four times a year, the bishops were bidden to anathematize those who failed to observe it, and the barons were enjoined to enforce its provisions.

Magna Carta was a thoroughly feudal document. It was chiefly a guarantee of rights for the barons, and gave no attention at all to serfs. Of its 63 provisions, all but 12 are now obsolete. But implicit in it was the idea that justice depended on the observance of law by all, including the king, and it opened the way to later extensions of freedom.

Article 12 forbade the levy of scutage (money paid by a vassal to his lord in lieu of military service) except by "general consent"; this would later be interpreted to mean that the king could raise no taxes without consent of the barons, and still later without consent of the commoners in Parliament. Article 20 declared that a freeman could be fined "only according to the measure of his offenses." Article 28 provided that no government official might seize "corn or other movable goods" without immediate payment; this would appear in the Fifth Amendment to the American Constitution as "nor shall private property be taken for public use without just compensation." Article 38 said that "no official shall place a man on trial . . . without producing credible witnesses to the truth" of the accusation. Article 39 provided that no one might be imprisoned or stripped of his rights without being judged by his peers; this would subsequently guarantee trial by jury for everyone. Article 60 declared: "Let all men of our kingdom, whether clergy or laymen, observe [these customs and liberties] similarly in their relations with their own men."

The reign of John's son Henry III saw a development no less portentous for English constitutional government. Henry repeatedly imposed taxes for military ventures against the Welsh and the French, and the barons grew weary of digging into their pockets. Simon de Montfort, Earl of Leicester, led a resistance movement. Wishing to have more than the aid of his fellow barons in his defiance of the King, he called a council in 1265 to which he summoned two knights from every shire and two burgesses from every town. He gave them no power, but he flattered their self-importance by inviting them at all. Simon's council did no more than declare the widespread distaste for high taxation and foreign embroilments, but Henry took a lesson from the incident. When he next wanted to raise new taxes, in 1268, he too summoned the knights and burgesses to ask their support, and the English Parliament was under way.

Before the close of the 13th Century, when Henry's son, Edward I, sat on the throne, Parliament (from the French *parler*, to speak) would be the keystone of English government: the maker of national policy, the tax-granting body and the chief molder of public opinion.

In France, as in England, government grew centralized, but whereas in England the barons united to bring the king under the law, in France the lords were intermittently at war with their neighbors, and while they feuded among themselves, the king emerged as lawmaker.

Toward the close of the 11th Century, when William the Conqueror was founding the nation-state in England, the French King Philip I ruled only a narrow strip of territory, the Ile de France, which ran from Paris to Orléans. But Paris was an international marketplace. Anyone wishing to trade there had to travel the roads or sail the rivers that Paris commanded, and pay a toll to do so, thus enriching the treasuries of Philip and his successors, Louis VI and Louis VII. These were the men who began consolidating the monarchy. They put down bandit raids on monasteries and maintained order in the towns, and both clergy and common folk gave them loyalty in return. Townspeople sought their aid against oppression by the merchants and the feudal lords, and finally the lords sought their arbitration in quarrels among themselves. The king's court therefore came to be an effective center of justice.

France emerged as a nation at the start of the 13th Century under Philip II, known as Philip Augustus. Through marriage, conquest and confiscation, he extended his realm from Cherbourg to the Pyrenees. He amassed a sizable treasury, paved the muddy streets of Paris and built the Louvre as a fortress to guard the Seine. He instituted the custom of sending royal agents out from his court to administer local territories, collect taxes for the Crown and try cases formerly tried by the feudal lords. In the north these men were called *baillis* (bailiffs) and in the south *sénéchaux* (stewards). They resembled the circuit judges that Henry I had sent through England in the previous century, but whereas Henry's judges were itinerant, Philip assigned a man to a district and kept him there several years. If the man proved himself an able civil servant, he got another assignment; if he did not, he was fired.

The centralization effected by Philip Augustus continued under Louis IX, called Saint Louis. He founded hospitals, asylums, and homes for the blind and for reformed prostitutes; and wherever he went he had people fed at public expense, sometimes waiting on them himself. A man of contrasts, he spent hours at prayer and built Sainte-Chapelle to house a dubious relic of the Crucifixion, yet he brought the clergy under civil jurisdiction.

Louis left local administration in the hands of the *sénéchaux* and *baillis*, but he added something more: he sent *enquêteurs* (inquisitors) from the royal court to hear the complaints of all subjects, whatever their rank. These men were not judges; they were good-will ambassadors. The people could go to them over the heads of the *baillis* and *sénéchaux* and air their grievances, which the *enquêteurs* reported back to the King. Louis would then redress the wrongs. Like the trial by inquest devised by Henry II in England in the previous century, Louis' system extended rights to the lesser classes and made manifest the monarch's concern for his subjects. By the end of his reign, in 1270, no part of the kingdom was without some tie to the royal government. Respect for its power, and affection for Louis, bred loyalty to the monarchy as an institution.

This was the situation that prevailed when Philip IV, known as "the Fair" for his handsome looks, ascended the throne in 1285. Philip surrounded himself with ministers of state and ran his government by committee. Unlike the counselors of earlier kings, the men who advised Philip came from neither the baronage nor the clergy, but from the ranks of law-school graduates. The law schools, like other institutions of learning, were undergo-

ing an intellectual revival. Justinian's Code of the laws of imperial Rome had been rediscovered in the West, and it had inspired as much excitement as Aristotle's philosophy. The Code had long been the subject of enthusiastic study at the law schools of Bologna, Montpellier and elsewhere; now it came to be applied to contemporary affairs.

Instead of building a body of law on local custom, as the English had done, Philip's lawyers built it on Roman theory. They interpreted Justinian's Code to mean that the king possessed absolute legal prerogatives in his kingdom, and that whatever he decreed had the force of law. By such reasoning Philip's men completed the centralization of royal power and tightened his rein over the feudal barons.

Philip created a general assembly of lords, clergy, knights and bourgeoisie, but, with his absolute authority, he gave it quite a different character from the Parliament in England. He summoned the assembly in 1302, to secure their support in a struggle with the papacy, and in 1314, to disclose his reasons for a new tax. In neither case did he ask advice or leave a decision to the delegates— they were there to hear his wishes—but he gained the appearance of seeking public support, and gave his people a sense of participation. Eventually the French assembly would come to be known as the *Etats-Généraux* (Estates-General), named for the three estates of the kingdom—nobles, clergy and commoners.

Centralized monarchy was slower to develop elsewhere than in England and France, but written laws and representative government spread all over Europe.

Events in Germany were linked with those in Italy, for from the 10th Century on, every German ruler had had an eye on Italian lands and a hand in Italian politics. Because these men neglected their rule at home for conquest in Italy or disputes with the popes, they failed to found a nation-state. Frederick Barbarossa, who reigned from 1152 to 1190, made some strides toward consolidating Germany but died before he could complete the job. The hereditary princes continued to rule their lands unbeholden to the King, and the towns were astir with rich and assertive burghers. In the east the barons built up small independent principalities; in the west the burghers formed leagues that checked baronial power. In both principalities and towns, however, legal and administrative systems developed that, though small and primitive compared with those of the French and English monarchies, kept a measure of peace and order among the citizens.

In the 13th Century Frederick II, the grandson of Frederick Barbarossa, reversed the usual German route. Intending to unite Italy with Germany, he began with Sicily, where he was born and raised (his mother was the daughter of the Sicilian King). In 1231 Frederick and his advisers drew up the Constitution of Melfi, taking their ideas from Justinian's Code as the lawyers of France were to do some 40 years later. The Constitution centralized all authority in Frederick as Emperor, forbade the nobles to make private war and excluded the clergy from public office. It provided for the prosecution of crimes that lax baronial rulers had theretofore left unpunished. It was the first medieval code to apply the principles of Roman law, the first to seek the prevention (as opposed to punishment) of crime, the first to institute a stable gold currency, and the first to standardize weights and measures. It abolished trial by ordeal, recognized female inheritance and protected serfs against abuse.

Frederick was as far ahead of his time in administration as in legislation. He appointed trained and salaried officials to govern for him. He put the grain trade, the exchange of money, the baths and the slaughterhouses under state control. He fos-

tered the cultivation of cotton and sugar cane, founded model farms and exterminated disease-bearing animals. He cleared forest lands for vineyards, sank wells, built bridges and paved roads. He raised Sicily to a level of prosperity unmatched by any European country of the time.

Frederick did not, however, succeed in uniting Italy with Germany, nor did he leave an enduring state. He spent very little time in Germany and it remained in the hands of the feudal princes. He devastated northern Italy by warring for control of its cities, and he incurred the wrath of the popes with his imperial designs. Both Gregory IX and Innocent IV excommunicated him and preached crusades against him. The Germanic empire in effect died with Frederick, and Italy continued in disorder. It would not be united under one rule until the 19th Century.

If Germany and Italy were slow to found the nation-state, they laid two other cornerstones on which the modern West is built: trade and technology. The inventiveness of Germanic technicians harnessed wind and water on a larger scale than any known before, produced machinery to do the work of human hands, and anticipated the Industrial Revolution of the 18th Century.

Mining had been practiced by the Romans, but it had fallen out of use during the early Middle Ages. One metal that continued to be worked was iron, which was needed for agricultural implements and arms. Then, gradually, Germany began to take advantage of its rich deposits of gold, silver and copper as well as iron. It had rushing mountain streams and plenty of timber for building fires. The Germans took the water mill—a device known to China, Rome and Islam, but used mainly for grinding grain—and put it to work in tandem with mining machinery. In the lowlands, where the streams froze in the cold of winter, the winds continued to blow; and there the windmill took

THE MECHANICAL CLOCK, *a medieval invention, had become a kind of universe in miniature by the 14th Century when the great Wells Cathedral clock was built in England. The face and original inner works are shown above. Four winds and their attendant angels surround the face, which tells not only the 24 hours of the day but also the days of the lunar month, pointed out by a crescent moon. (The minutes are a later addition.) At center, the moon goddess Phoebe looks out, while to the right the moon's phases are shown.*

the place of the water mill. By the early 14th Century there were mills that drove the tools for fulling cloth, tanning leather, sawing wood, crushing ore; for operating the bellows of blast furnaces, the hammers of forges, the grindstones to finish and polish weapons and armor; for reducing pigment for paint and mash for beer.

When medieval mining first began, the landowners claimed the yield of the mines and used their serfs to work them. In the middle of the 12th Century Frederick Barbarossa declared that the sovereign had sole rights to the mines, and all mining thereafter was done under state control. In England the Crown claimed gold and silver deposits, but allowed other metals to be mined privately, provided royalties were paid to the king. Italian bankers financed the mining operations, and kings and queens and the wealthy bourgeoisie invested in them.

Germany sold its products and taught its techniques to all the rest of Europe. When in 1551 Spain reopened a silver and lead mine that had lain unused under the Moorish occupation, it sent to Germany for 200 Germans skilled in mining. Under Elizabeth I England, too, called on Germany for technicians and laborers, and Norway did the same when it opened a silver mine at Kongsberg in 1623.

Medieval men were fascinated with the effects of color and light—witness the stained-glass cathedral windows—and it was they who developed the optical lens, possibly through the accidental discovery of an anonymous Venetian glassmaker. Eyeglasses were in use in Italy in the 13th Century. In the later centuries other craftsmen would refine the lens, and from it fashion the telescope and the microscope.

Science as such was scarcely practiced in medieval times, but the scientific method was articulated for the first time in the 13th Century by Roger

Bacon, a Franciscan monk who taught at the University of Paris and at Oxford. Bacon chided his contemporaries for their obeisance to Aristotle—not, like the archconservatives of his day, out of opposition to heresy, but because he perceived the importance of first-hand experiment and investigation. If only men would study the world around them instead of poring over the works of antiquity, he declared, science would outdo the wonders of magic. "Machines may be made," he predicted, "by which the largest ships, with only one man steering them, will be moved faster than if they were filled with rowers; wagons may be built which will move with incredible speed and without the aid of beasts; flying machines can be constructed in which a man . . . may beat the air with wings like a bird . . . machines will make it possible to go to the bottom of seas and rivers."

Medicine during the early medieval era had been largely associated with magic, and disease with the wrath of God. But the Crusades and Italian trade with the Near East acquainted Europe with Arabic drugs, and in the 11th Century medical schools—seven of them in Italy alone—began to teach Greek, Arabic and Hebrew medicine.

As the practice of medicine spread, health and disease came to be public concerns. As early as the first half of the 12th Century, a state license was required for the practice of medicine in Sicily. A century later, under Frederick II, the aspiring physician could earn it only after five years of study, two examinations by the medical school at Salerno, and a term of practice under the supervision of a licensed physician. Also in the 13th Century health ordinances began to be enacted in increasing numbers. Many cities paid physicians to treat the poor, and those in Spain required physicians to make periodic examinations of all citizens. In the 14th Century the towns in Flanders enforced laws dealing with the cleanliness of food and water.

Perhaps the greatest public-health achievement of the Middle Ages was the development of hospitals, which proliferated all over Europe in the 13th Century. The first hospitals were of whitewashed wood; later they were two- and three-story marble-pillared buildings around open courtyards, elaborately decorated like the palaces of the day. The first were founded by monasteries, but with the rise of the bourgeoisie and secular rule, kings and queens and bankers founded and endowed them, and city administrations ran them. The early hospitals were built outside the city walls to separate infectious patients from the rest of the population.

St. Bartholomew's, which was founded in London in 1123 by a Norman monk, was the first hospital to have a royal charter. Although its original buildings have been replaced, it stands on the same site. The Hôtel-Dieu in Paris has remained in the same location, near Notre-Dame, since the end of the 12th Century. Santa Maria Nuova, founded in Florence in 1287 by the father of Dante's Beatrice, was of such wide repute that the King of England and the Pope sent for copies of its regulations. By 1300 Florence had 30 hospitals and beds for more than a thousand patients.

As the 14th Century dawned, the results of the medieval flowering were everywhere apparent—in politics, economy, technology and social services. Medieval man had institutions to mete out justice and allow him to live in peace with his neighbor. He could send his sons to school. He had freedom to better his place in society, and institutions that would make society better for his descendants. He had skills to manufacture comforts unknown to his forebears, and he earned the money to buy them. He had hospitals to care for the poor and the old, and the beginnings of medical science. He had reached a peak of civilization. Misfortune, however, hovered just beyond the crest.

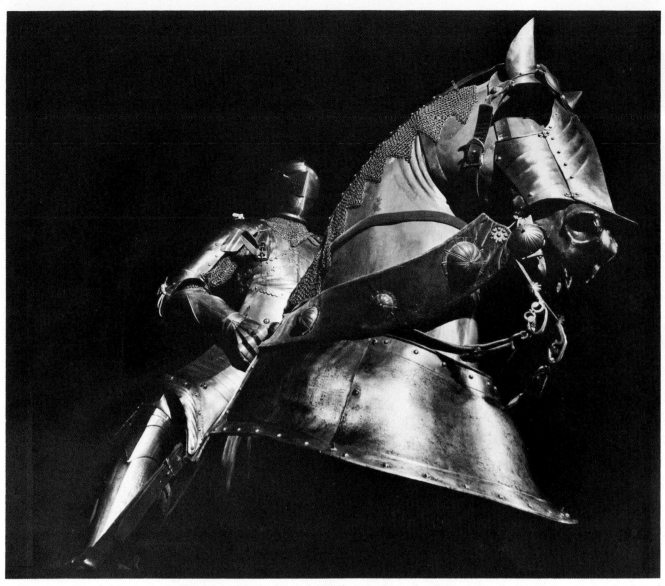

HORSE AND RIDER, *clad in armor, dominated warfare in the High Middle Ages. Many knights rode into battle wearing 60 pounds of steel.*

MEN IN ARMOR

Much of the history of the Middle Ages is summed up in the rise and fall of the epoch's cavalry—the knights in armor. These warriors first learned of the horse's value painfully, fighting against mounted barbarians. In the following centuries, the knightly horsemen exploited their mounts' speed and momentum to establish absolute mastery over the battlefield, terrorizing foot soldiers with their headlong charges. But in the 14th Century the infantrymen, using more powerful weapons and better tactics, broke the horsemen's domination in key battles. Vainly the cavalry sacrificed mobility for the added protection of heavier armor *(above)*. Before gunpowder wrote a thunderous epitaph to the medieval style of warfare, the horseman and the feudal system which supported him were on the decline.

Hastings: The Horseman Enthroned as Lord of Battles

The horseman's superiority over foot soldiers was proved conclusively near the English town of Hastings on October 14, 1066, when Norman invaders led by Duke William attacked King Harold's Saxon army. The battle, illustrated here with scenes from the 11th Century Bayeux Tapestry, was fought out between forces that seemed equal. Each army had roughly 5,000 men. The enemies were similarly armed, with swords, lances and short bows, and they wore the same basic battle garment—a coat of mail, which might consist of 250,000 steel rings.

There was one real difference between the two forces: the Norman army had many horsemen. Their charges finally wore down the Saxons and made William England's King. With this victory, the cavalry began a reign that would last 300 years.

NORMAN HORSEMEN *carrying lances set out from Hastings to attack King Harold's Saxon infantrymen. The Normans, under William the Conqueror, began their assault on Harold "before his army was arrayed."*

CECI DE

MAN-TO-MAN COMBAT *between a Norman on horseback and a Saxon on foot clearly shows the rider's advantage at close quarters. The mounted swordsman, slashing from above, outreaches and strikes down his opponent.*

SAXON FOOT SOLDIERS, *hurling their missiles, face Norman riders at Hastings. A chronicler wrote, "King Harold was slain there . . . and many good men, and the Frenchmen had possession of the place of slaughter."*

Courtrai: A Fateful Triumph
for Citizen Infantry

To cut down the horsemen's advantage, the foot soldiers improved their weapons. The short bow, effective only to about 50 yards, was superseded by the crossbow *(right)*, whose shafts could pierce mail at 200 yards, and by the longbow, which could shoot as far as the crossbow and five times faster. The eight-foot-long halberd and other staff weapons proved useful in checking a cavalry charge.

Through the 13th Century the horseman maintained his sway, gradually reinforcing his mail with more and more plates of form-fitting steel. But the new infantry weapons, wielded by determined, well-trained men, put an end to the cavalry's dominance in the 14th Century.

The battle that started the horseman's decline was fought in 1302 at Courtrai in Flanders. Here a Flemish force of 7,400 citizen foot soldiers faced a magnificent French army of 50,000 men, most of them mounted. The cavalrymen, trapped on marshy ground and weighed down with armor, perished by the thousands. From the dead the townsmen collected a portentous booty—2,000 golden spurs.

FLEMISH INFANTRYMEN, *battling the French near the town of Courtrai, bring down an elegant horseman with their spiked clubs. A Flemish artisan-soldier carved this scene on a wood chest after the smashing victory.*

A GIANT CROSSBOW, *so powerful that it had to be drawn mechanically, is aimed at its prime medieval target, horsemen's armor. At the rear stand staff weapons used against cavalry: a halberd (left) and a war hammer.*

BOMBARDING ORLEANS, *English soldiers behind a siege wall (left) fire their cannon across the Loire River into the French town—with little effect.*

Orléans: A Noisy Overture to Modern Warfare

Long sieges of fortified places occurred more often than major battles, and frequently produced more lasting results. The development of siege warfare, paralleling the struggle between cavalry and infantry, was an epoch-long contest between the offense and the defense. The attackers fashioned powerful catapults; one gigantic slingshot, weighing four tons, hurled a 60-pound rock 500 yards. The defenders built their walls 15 to 30 feet thick, and from atop these ramparts they showered the enemy with arrows, boulders and boiling oil. In turn the attackers made movable shelters to protect them as

they stormed the citadel. When all else failed, the attackers might surround the defensive walls with walls of their own, then spend a year or two starving the garrison into surrender.

A new siege weapon, the cannon, made its debut around 1350. Cannon were used by both sides during the English siege of Orléans (above) in 1428-1429. But the effective use of gunpowder still lay in the future. It was not the French cannon that broke the siege of Orléans and turned the Hundred Years' War in France's favor. It was the arrival of a relief force led by an armored warrior—Joan of Arc.

A PRIMITIVE CANNON, *cast in the 15th Century, stands strapped to a wooden chassis. The gun was loaded with stone cannon balls, seen at right; its powder charge was ignited by a red-hot rod.*

8

WINDS OF CHANGE

To all outward appearances, the 14th Century in medieval Europe opened on a note of triumph. At its very start, in 1300, Pope Boniface VIII proclaimed a Jubilee to celebrate the new centenary of Christ's birth. In overwhelming response, joyous multitudes poured into the Eternal City. The size of the throngs—estimated at two million for the year—compelled the unprecedented use of traffic rules on Rome's narrow bridges. The generosity of the gifts and offerings, heaped upon the altars, created a pleasanter problem. At St. Paul's, one chronicler reported, two priests were kept busy night and day "raking together infinite money."

The Church and the faithful alike had cause to feel that the Jubilee year augured well for the decades to come. In the two centuries past, medieval people had progressed beyond all expectation, and the papacy had reached a new peak of power. Boniface had before him the example of Innocent III, a Pope so skilled at asserting his supremacy over emperors and kings that he had humbled five of them by excommunication or interdict. Boniface assumed that he could continue on the same path. But within three years of the Jubilee he was to die of the shock of the greatest personal insult ever to be inflicted upon a pontiff. The anticipations of lesser men would also be jolted. Famine, war, plague, peasants' revolts, disorder within the Church—troubles of many sorts were to disrupt European life. Even as Jubilee celebrants rejoiced, forces were at work which marked the beginning of the end of the Middle Ages.

Politically, medieval people were adrift somewhere between the old moorings of feudalism and the new moorings of centralized monarchy. Economically, each stratum of society had its reasons for dissatisfaction. Bourgeois entrepreneurs felt hemmed in by jealously localized trade practices. Less well-to-do townsfolk resented the widening gap between merchants and artisans. Serfs who had seen their fellows leave the manor for the town were restive. The feudal noble faced ruination. Cold cash was what he now needed to keep himself in fine clothes and armor, and cold cash was what he notably lacked. Many aristocrats were reduced to "gentleman beggars." In France, some manor houses came to be known as "châteaux de la misère."

ST. FRANCIS OF ASSISI, *in a fresco by the 13th Century Italian master Cimabue, is shown with the marks of the Crucifixion on his hands. The wounds appeared, it is said, after the saint had seen a vision of Christ crucified.*

In a money economy, money talked. Increasingly men at the top of the medieval power structure realized that they had to command ever-larger sources of revenue. This, in turn, required a broader authority to tax. The struggle over this issue, between the Church and the brash national monarchies of England and France, touched off the turmoil of the 14th Century.

The throne of England was occupied by Edward I, the throne of France by Philip the Fair. Both were strong, self-assured personalities, and at odds with each other over lands in France still under English control. To finance their costly campaigns, Edward and Philip hit upon the same solution: a tax on the clergy within their realms. But—in the Church view—Church revenues were exempt from compulsory assessments, and taxable only by the Church.

In 1296 Boniface VIII issued *Clericis laicos,* a bull threatening excommunication for any lay ruler who taxed the clergy and any churchman who paid without papal consent. But Edward and Philip were a new breed of secular monarch, unimpressed by fulminations from Rome. Edward's retort was to decree that if the clergy did not pay, they were to be shorn of all legal protection, and their temporal property was to be seized by the King's sheriffs. Philip's answer was to place a complete embargo on the export of all gold, silver and jewels from his domains, thus depriving the papal coffers of a major fount of revenue from Church collections in France. Boniface soon gave way. He explained that he had not meant to proscribe clerical contributions for defense in times of dire need. Since the Kings could decide what constituted "defense" and "dire need," the victory for Edward and Philip was clear.

It was not yet complete, however. Buoyed by the smashing success of the Jubilee year, Boniface concluded that the spiritual obeisance it manifested for him in every corner of Christendom extended to the temporal sphere as well. Concentrating his fire upon Philip, the Pope proceeded to try to teach him his place. In 1301 the King imprisoned a French bishop—a former papal legate—on charges of treason. Boniface ordered the prelate's release and rescinded his earlier concession on clerical taxation. Philip's response, in 1302, was to summon representatives of the French nobility, clergy and bourgeoisie—the debut of his national assembly, the Estates-General—and elicit their unanimous support in his quarrel with the Pope. One of Philip's ministers put the choice baldly. "My master's sword is made of steel," he commented. "The Pope's is made of verbiage."

Several months later Boniface issued *Unam sanctam,* the most extreme assertion of papal temporal supremacy in all Church history. This time Boniface made his meaning unmistakable. "It is altogether necessary," he declared, "for every human being to be subject to the Roman pontiff." The King's countermaneuver was no less drastic. He prepared to have Boniface deposed on the ground that his election had been illegal. To prosecute this task he chose William of Nogaret, one of the shrewdest of the lawyers who were helping Philip build the foundations for his nation-state.

Nogaret was also a master of the trumped-up charge. He had been known to approve the use of "voluntary" testimony obtained by such means as stripping a witness, smearing him with honey and hanging him over a beehive. Nogaret's bill of particulars against Boniface grew to include not only the illegitimacy of his election, but heresy, simony and immorality. Armed with authority from an assembly of French prelates and nobles to bring the Pope to France for trial before a special Church council, he sped to Italy. Boniface, now 86, had left the heat of Rome to summer in the foothills of the Apennines at his birthplace, Anagni. Nogaret and some troops he had marshaled broke in on the aged pontiff in his bedroom. Whether they actually manhandled him is in dispute. That they heaped imprecations upon him there is no doubt. Boniface was kept prisoner for several days. At last the plain people of Anagni rose up and rescued him. Numbed and humiliated, he died within weeks.

Anagni came to symbolize the nadir of papal power even as Canossa, some two centuries before, had symbolized its zenith. When Boniface's successor in Rome died after a brief, ineffectual reign, Philip's daring coup bore its fruit. In 1305 the College of Cardinals elected a Frenchman, Clement V, as Pope. Clement never set foot in Rome, preferring to stay closer to home, where he was always accessible to royal bidding.

Clement's election marked the start of the 72-year period in Church history called—after the long exile of the ancient Jews in Babylon—the Babylonian Captivity. Following Clement, six successive Popes, all of French origin, chose not to reside in Rome. Avignon, on the Rhone River just across from the borders of Philip's domain, became the site of the Holy See. From a small town, Avignon grew into a busy city of 80,000, with all the panoply of an immense clerical bureaucracy and with a sumptuous papal palace. The forte of the Avignon popes was financial and administrative. The spiritual guidance they offered seemed somehow dilute; the voice of the Vicar of Christ had a less majestic ring from Avignon than from the Eternal City. Having witnessed the degradation of the papacy, now watching its incumbents settle under the thumb of the French monarchy, Europeans grew hardened. They were weary of church-state strife, and other troubles engrossed them.

Among these was the start in 1337 of the Hundred Years' War between England and France. Except as a chronological convenience, the title is a misnomer. The war was neither continuous nor full-scale but rather a number of disjointed campaigns, essentially a continuation of the fighting in which the English and French had engaged off and on ever since 1066. The reasons for bad blood between the two countries were many. Their seafarers clashed over pirating practices in the Channel. Their sovereigns quarreled over feudal homage due for lands held by the English in France. French kings gave military aid and comfort to Scotland, a perennial thorn in England's side. English kings rallied to Flanders, the traditional market for English wool, against attempted encroachments by the French.

Added to these older sources of friction was the cocky spirit of the new nationalism. To the men on the English and French thrones, the notion of national aggrandizement was far from displeasing. When Philip the Fair's youngest son died, the direct Capetian line of French kings died with him, and the throne went to a cousin, Philip VI. Thereupon Edward III of England, whose mother was a daughter of Philip the Fair, laid claim to the French crown. To the lions on his royal coat of arms he added the French fleur-de-lis, and personally headed an invasion force into Normandy.

The initial phase of the war saw a battle dear to the heart of every Englishman since. It took place at Crécy, due north of Paris, in 1346. Although the French army far outnumbered the English, Edward had a deadly surprise in store. Flanking his knights were archers armed with a devastating weapon, the longbow. The French forces also included archers —Genoese mercenaries—but the familiar crossbows they were using were outclassed. The longbow could shoot yard-long arrows a distance of almost 400 yards at the rate of five to six arrows a minute, compared to one for the crossbow. The English poured arrows into the ranks of enemy horsemen so fast that, according to the chronicle of Froissart, "they fell like snow."

Crécy brought a great surge of national pride

among Edward's subjects. The war found wide favor with them. Understandably, the French viewed it with loathing. Added to the usual ravages of warfare was a newer kind of calamity. Both armies had recruited soldiers who fought for pay rather than under the old feudal concept of service. Between battles, both English soldier and Genoese hireling roamed the land with all the gusto of the early barbarians. Large areas of France were laid waste. Crops and houses were burned, property picked clean and the inhabitants made penniless—when they were not wantonly killed.

While France reeled and England rejoiced, a catastrophe of unprecedented proportions awaited them both, and all the rest of the Continent as well. Out of the East came a terrible pestilence. Medical historians now believe that it was a variety of the bubonic plague. Contemporary accounts labelled it the Black Death, because of the dark skin blotches which heralded its onset. The Black Death dispatched its sufferers after an agonized interim of one to three days in which they spewed up blood, fell into delirium, and broke out in boils, carbuncles, and lumps the size of eggs.

Medieval writers ascribed responsibility for the plague to the Mongol hordes which had swept west from Asia and were besieging the Genoese trading station of Kaffa on the Black Sea. Among Asians, the plague was no stranger. Whenever a soldier succumbed, his corpse would be catapulted over Kaffa's walls. Rats carried the disease aboard homeward-bound Italian vessels, and in April 1348 it struck in Florence. Later that year it overran the rest of Italy and France. England's turn came in 1349, Germany's and Scandinavia's in 1350. Estimates of the toll range from one fourth to one half of Europe's entire population.

The effects of war were as a pinprick compared with the tragic consequences of the plague. Food supplies ran short because, in many places, there was no one left to cultivate the soil or to supervise the cultivators. Commercial enterprises slumped. Schools, universities and charitable services shut down for lack of qualified personnel to run them. Crafts suffered irretrievable losses through the death of guild masters who could pass their skills on to apprentices. The sharp break in continuity extended to the most basic institutions; for decades afterward, litigants in court cases were not expected to be familiar with the old unwritten laws that had governed their fathers and grandfathers.

The dimensions of the disaster compelled the widespread conviction that the plague represented divine retribution for human sins. Many Europeans, disenchanted by Avignon, already tended to be introverted and individual in their faith. The fright and horror stirred by the plague now sent them to extremes. Some lost faith completely and formed cults for the worship of Satan. Others indulged in frenzies of religious excess. Many joined the Flagellants, who believed that they could be purged of sin, and thus escape punishment from on high, by flogging themselves with leather scourges studded with iron spikes. Other Europeans sought solace in superstition, personal revelations and mystical ecstasies. A morbid fascination grew for the grotesque, the revolting and the necrophilic. Treatises on the *Ars moriendi*, the art of dying, became immensely popular.

The plague also cast a long shadow in the form of social unrest. In a number of European countries the previously well-ordered structure of medieval society began to be shaken by violent uprisings by peasants and artisans against nobles and wealthy merchants.

France saw the first major eruption. The French had scarcely begun to assess the shattering impact of the Black Death when they had to contend with a new English invasion in the southwest. In 1356, at Poitiers, French forces suffered a defeat as com-

THE DANCE OF DEATH, *printed in 1486, was a favorite theme in that era of war, plague and famine. Here, with macabre glee, skeletons snatch a bishop and a noble; other versions showed poor peasants achieving equality with the rich in death.*

plete as at Crécy in 1346. Edward III had put his troops in the charge of his eldest son, Edward, called the Black Prince because of the black armor he habitually wore. Using the same general strategy his father had devised at Crécy, the Prince added a stunning success of his own. He captured the French King, Philip VI's son, John II, and carried him off to London.

The French government was in disarray, and the pent-up wrath of the lower classes exploded. The Dauphin of France, ruling in his father's absence, had to flee Paris after a mob had forced him into the indignity of donning a cap with the red and blue colors of the popular opposition. Far more ruinous events rocked the countryside to the north, in an uprising known as the Jacquerie, for Jacques, the nickname of the peasant. Jacques nursed a special fury of his own, directed at the local lord who, although he had failed to shield his tenants from the destruction of war and the depredations of mercenaries, blandly continued to insist on his usual rents and services.

Banding together, peasants put the torch to manor houses and set upon their masters. But staves and scythes were no match for swords and lances. The insurrection was crushed, and brutal reprisals

followed in short order. Known troublemakers were hanged outside their own cottages and entire villages were razed.

The same spirit of rebellion lurked in England. The plague had created a critical shortage of farm labor. Surviving peasants were emboldened to ask for higher wages. If they were refused, they deserted to new employers who would meet their price. Parliament, composed largely of landholders, was aghast. In 1351 it approved a Statute of Laborers decreeing imprisonment for anyone who refused to work for the wages prevailing before the plague. Neither this nor a subsequent string of similar laws won much compliance. But resentment over their attempted enforcement simmered, and began to boil up when the tide turned against the English in the war with the French.

The chief architect of this military reversal was a brilliant Breton general, Bertrand du Guesclin. The same Dauphin who had been mocked by a Paris mob now sat on the throne as Charles V. In 1369 the people under the repressive rule of the Black Prince in southwestern France appealed to Charles for help. Confident of his military commander, Charles renewed the war. By the time of his death in 1380, his judgment had been fully borne out. In 10 years Du Guescelin had driven the English from virtually all their territories in France except the ports of Calais, Bordeaux and Bayonne.

It was England's turn to loathe the war and watch its government flounder. Edward III, the hero of Crécy, had died in his dotage in 1377; his son, the Black Prince, had died a year earlier. The Prince's son, Richard II, was only 10 when he was crowned, and ruled under the guidance of a 12-man council. To help prosecute the war, Parliament imposed a new kind of poll, or head, tax. Unless he were a total pauper, every Englishman was required to pay.

For the lower classes, the poll tax proved the final straw. Open revolt flared in 1381. Under an ex-soldier named Wat Tyler, rebels of Kent and Essex marched on London. Sympathetic artisans opened the gates, and the newcomers ran amok. Among the high dignitaries they murdered was the Archbishop of Canterbury; among the mansions they burned was that of the King's uncle, John of Gaunt. After three days of terror, the rebels confronted the King himself. Richard, now 14, went into their midst and promised to meet all their demands, including more equitable rents and taxes and the abolition of the tenure of serfdom. But at a second parley the next day, one of the royal escort slew Wat Tyler. The revolt collapsed. Tyler's followers were permitted to go home. Their demands were unfulfilled and, as in the earlier French uprising, retribution by local lords awaited them.

Rebellion, nevertheless, had its lasting effects. No more in medieval times would a poll tax be levied. Serfdom would gradually die out. Even more significant, the serf in the country and the artisan in town had forged a bond; the lower classes had given expression to their grievances in words and deeds. Out of the English uprising came one of the most notable declarations of human equality ever voiced. Its author was a Kentish priest, John Ball. The gentry called him mad, but the people listened. "By what right are they whom we call lords greater folk than we?" Ball asked. "If we all came of the same father and mother, of Adam and Eve, how can they say or prove that they are better than we, if it be not that they make us gain for them by our toil what they spend in their pride?" In the retelling, Ball's preachment was condensed to a simple verse: "When Adam delved and Eve span, who was then the gentleman?"

However effective, Ball's influence was minor compared to that of John Wycliffe, a teacher at Oxford. Wycliffe fanned the flames of egalitarianism not on social but on religious grounds. Every man's salvation, he argued, rested on his own faith and behavior. Wycliffe not only challenged the clergy's authority to administer the sacraments but also denied the truth of the doctrine of transubstantiation, which declares that all the bread and all the wine used in the Mass become the whole body and blood of Christ as a result of the words of consecration. Wycliffe asserted that the believer did not partake of Christ's body, but communed with Him in spirit, through personal faith. An individual did not need the Church to guide him in matters of religious belief and practice; he could consult the Bible directly. Pursuing his doctrine, Wycliffe and his followers produced an English translation of the Bible so the people could read for themselves.

For a time Wycliffe enjoyed elite as well as popular support. As a corollary of his theories, he urged that the Church divest itself, or be divested, of its worldly wealth, and once more embrace the poverty of the Apostles. For years Englishmen had watched the outflow of English gold and silver to support the papacy at Avignon—and, they suspected, to help finance the French campaigns against them. Parliament had tried to nullify the supranational power of the popes, financial and otherwise, by a law in 1351 which in effect barred the appoint-

ment of foreigners to Church benefices in England, and by a law in 1353 which forbade appeals of cases from English to foreign courts. Neither statute, however, prevented Avignon from the continued enjoyment of its English resources. In 1376 a Parliamentary report indicated that the taxes levied by the Pope in England totaled five times those collected by the King.

Wycliffe's proposal to deprive the Church of property not used for religious purposes brought him influential admirers all too willing to help in the proposed seizure. But few would go along with such unorthodoxy as his attack on transubstantiation. He lost still more support in high places after the Peasants' Revolt, which he was accused of helping foment. Wycliffe's works were condemned and he left Oxford. He died in 1384, implacably turning out tracts to the end.

He left his imprint on many people in many places. His countrymen now had their own Bible, and considerable food for thought. In far-off Bohemia two scholars, Jerome of Prague and Jan Hus, took up some of Wycliffe's beliefs and spread them through Central Europe, where the Protestant Ref-

ormation would be born a century or so hence. Within the Church itself men recognized the danger signals and the need to revitalize the faith.

A step in that direction had been taken with Gregory XI's move back to Rome from Avignon in 1377. Joy over the re-establishment of the Holy See in the Eternal City was short-lived. Gregory's death within a year necessitated a new papal election. The College of Cardinals, still heavily weighted with Frenchmen, yielded to the clamor of a Roman mob and chose an Italian, Urban VI. Then, however, the French cardinals declared the proceedings invalid because of intimidation. From their own number they chose another Pope, Clement VII. Urban ruled from Rome; Clement from Avignon.

Thus began the bleak chapter in Church annals known as the Great Schism. It lasted for 39 years. Each Pope had his own College of Cardinals, thereby insuring the papal succession to a suitable choice. Each Pope claimed to be the true Vicar of Christ, with the power to excommunicate those who did not acknowledge him.

Periodic attempts to heal the breach foundered over such questions as which Pope had the right to call a Church council. Some of the rival cardinals united long enough to arrange a conclave at Pisa in 1409, at which both Popes were deposed and a new one elected. But neither deposed Pope would accept the verdict. The papacy now had not two, but three, incumbents.

This bizarre denouement discomfited Europe sufficiently to goad its leaders into firm action. From 1414 to 1418 the German city of Constance played host to a great international council attended not only by prelates, but by representatives of kings and princes acting in the specific name and interests of their own nations. At length the Council got one papal incumbent to abdicate, deposed the other two, and chose a new pontiff, Martin V. One of the deposed Popes, Benedict XIII of Avignon, clung to his claim, but to all practical purposes, Constance ended the Great Schism.

While the Council was still in session, another of medieval Europe's major dilemmas, the Hundred Years' War, began to be resolved. In 1415 hostilities were renewed by England's strutting young King Henry V. At Agincourt, not far from the scene of his great-grandfather's triumph at Crécy, similar strategy and the same fateful longbow again bested the French. Proceeding through Normandy, Harry had a formidable ally in the Duke of Burgundy, a kinsman but bitter enemy of Charles VI, the weakling French monarch. Charles, noted for his deranged behavior, put on one of his oddest performances after the Burgundians captured Paris. He disowned his own son, married off his daughter to Henry and made him his heir.

The way seemed clear for a complete English take-over in France. Both Charles and Henry died less than two years after they had made their curious pact. Henry's infant son, Henry VI, was acclaimed King of both countries. A royal uncle, the Duke of Bedford, confidently laid siege to the city of Orléans, the gateway to central and southern France, which were still unsubdued.

It was here that a lowly peasant girl intervened to alter history. Joan of Arc became convinced that she heard the voices of saints urging her to save her country. Leaving her native village in Lorraine, she made her way through areas controlled by the English and the Burgundians to Chinon, the headquarters of the disinherited son of Charles VI. She told the younger Charles of her divine mission. Impressed but cautious, Charles first had some theologians examine her for signs of witchcraft. When they pronounced her pure, he sent her on to Orléans with a few troops.

Frenchmen ever after would glory and grieve over Joan's subsequent fortunes. Wearing a man's armor and riding a white horse, she so inspired her soldiers and the beleaguered people of Orléans that the siege was raised and the English routed in short order. On July 17, 1429, she stood near the Dauphin as he was crowned Charles VII in the great cathedral at Rheims. Months later the Burgundians captured her and sold her to the English. Under English pressure, a Church court found her guilty of heresy. The man whose throne she had secured made no effort to save her. In 1431, the Maid of Orléans was burned at the stake in the marketplace of Rouen.

After a quarter-century the Church reversed her sentence, and after five centuries recognized her as a saint; her canonization came in 1920. But the countrymen to whom she had taught the meaning of patriotism passed their own judgment on her. Imbued with her courage, they began to push the invaders back. When the Hundred Years' War ceased in 1453, the English held only Calais.

The winds of change blew everywhere. That same year the Turks took Constantinople. Blocked at one end of the Mediterranean, Europeans increasingly turned the opposite way. In 1456 doughty Portuguese sailors, venturing into the Atlantic some 400 miles out of sight of land, discovered the Cape Verde Islands, encouraging a Genoese named Columbus to make a more distant journey a few decades later.

At home Europeans expanded their horizons without stirring, thanks to the proliferation of a new machine, the printing press, devised in a shop in the Rhineland. The second half of the 15th Century saw the birth of Niccolò Machiavelli, who would transform men's ideas of politics and statecraft; of Martin Luther, who would revolutionize their ideas of religion; of Leonardo da Vinci and Michelangelo Buonarroti, who would elevate their ideas of art. The Middle Ages had run their course, but the soil they had prepared would nourish generations to come.

A LIVELY TOWNSWOMAN *carved on Jacques Coeur's mansion in Bourges, France, gazes at the bustling street below.*

ENDURING MONUMENTS OF AN AGE

Despite the ravages of the centuries, medieval buildings survive in great numbers, revealing the variety and vitality of life in the Middle Ages. Every human activity from warfare to worship can be seen in the structures on the following pages—castles, guildhalls, a pilgrimage church. Profound social changes also are reflected in these buildings. The palatial town house that displays the statue above attests to the creation of a great new class, the bourgeoisie. Jacques Coeur, who built the mansion in the 1440s, was a merchant, yet without benefit of noble birth or clerical rank he became the richest and most powerful man in Europe. His house—and today's middle class—confirm the success of the radical new outlook expressed in Coeur's motto: "For the valiant heart, nothing is impossible."

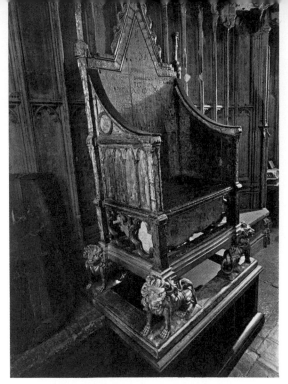

A CORONATION THRONE, *used for the installation of English monarchs since 1308, stands in Westminster Abbey.*

Safer Thrones, Finer Castles

The growth of royal power left a clear record in the changing styles of military architecture. In early times, when thrones were shaky seats, monarchs built massive fortresses like Dover Castle (*below*), not only to repulse foreign invaders but also to defend themselves against sporadic attacks by their own rebellious noblemen. Gradually, however, the king's authority prevailed and baronial warfare diminished. The new security permitted lords to consider comfort in planning their strongholds. Later castles such as Bodiam (*opposite*) combined sophisticated defenses with well-organized living quarters and a refined, romantic elegance.

A FORTIFIED MANORHOUSE, *both home and stronghold for a lord, Bodiam Castle rises in an artificial lake. Bodiam was constructed in 1385 to offer "resistance against our enemies," the French, but it never saw action.*

AN IMPREGNABLE FORTRESS—*a medieval historian called it "the key of England"—Dover Castle crowns a snow-dusted height guarding the English Channel. Built for defense, Dover withstood its last real attack in 1216.*

A Prosperity Based on River Highways

Waterways were the main thoroughfares of the Middle Ages, and many a town owed its growth to river-borne commerce. Florence, on the Arno River, grew so fast that between 1220 and 1252 it built three bridges; in 1345 it replaced still another with the Ponte Vecchio *(below)*, now famous for its jewelers' shops. But Europe's busiest river was the Rhine. To exploit its enormous trade, many toll stations sprang up: by 1300, merchant craft on the Rhine were being taxed at more than 35 places. One such station, the island castle of Pfalz *(opposite)*, was still collecting tolls in the 19th Century.

GUARDING THE RHINE, *Pfalz castle, a former toll station, juts up on a bleak island. Because many such stations were run by clerics, the Rhine was dubbed "priests' lane."*

BRIDGING THE ARNO, *the Ponte Vecchio links two sections of Florence. The shops on the bridge once housed butchers, but civic pride demanded their ouster in the Renaissance.*

A RENDEZVOUS FOR MERCHANTS, *the guildhalls and depot buildings of wealthy old Ghent are reflected in the Lys River at the Graslei, the Wharf of*

Herbs. Wheat shipped by river from France was stored in the Granary, a 13th Century building seen here to the right of the tall steeple (center).

The Distinctive Towns of Merchants and Noblemen

The skyline of a medieval town often revealed its character—and its fate. In the towns of northern Italy, noblemen living in close quarters erected lofty towers for protection against their quarrelsome neighbors. The towers of San Gimignano *(opposite)* are reminders of that town's downfall: in the 14th Century, while feuding aristocrats were shooting at each other from atop their bastions, the town lost its liberty to Florence and began to decline.

The Flemish textile town of Ghent, by contrast, faced rising competition from England's woolen industry. Ghent met this economic threat by greatly expanding its trade in grain. To handle the added business, Ghent built more of the distinctive structures that identified it as a merchants' town—guildhalls and warehouses with steplike façades *(above)*.

AN ELABORATE CREST *identifies Ghent's Spice and Herb Merchants' Hall with the guild's symbolic mortar and pestles, plus the word "Kruideniers," which is the hall's name in Flemish.*

A BIZARRE BATTLEGROUND, *San Gimignano bristles with 15 martial towers, built by lords vying to possess the loftiest stronghold. The highest, marking the mayor's palace (center), rises 177 feet.*

173

MEDIEVAL STUDENTS *listen to a lecturer (left) in this relief at Notre Dame cathedral, where the University of Paris first held classes.*

A Robust Tradition of Academic Boldness

Medieval universities, starting in the 12th Century, established hardy traditions even before they got permanent quarters. The oldest university buildings still standing were begun at Merton College, Oxford, in 1264; Merton also acquired England's first university library *(opposite)* in the 1370s. By then, several European schools were famed for specialized courses: Bologna for the law; Salerno for medicine; Paris for theology. By then, too, students were writing home their ageless appeal: "I am studying . . . with the greatest diligence, but the matter of money stands greatly in the way . . ." A classic criticism of students had already been voiced by a French cleric: "Some studied merely to acquire knowledge, which is curiosity; others to acquire fame, which is vanity; others still for the sake of gain. . . . Very few studied for their own edification, or that of others." But in spite of student problems, the vigorous universities of the Middle Ages established a precedent of inestimable value to later generations: they firmly asserted for all time the principle of free intellectual inquiry.

PRECIOUS MANUSCRIPTS *repose in the 14th Century library of Merton College, Oxford. Books were hard to come by in the Middle Ages, and were often chained in place for safekeeping.*

THE PILGRIM'S GOAL, *Mont-Saint-Michel looms in the distance. Before the causeway was built in 1879 the shrine was inaccessible by land during high tide.*

Mont-Saint-Michel: The Soaring Spirit of an Era

THE CHURCH'S REFLECTION *ripples in the sea at ebb tide. By a prodigious engineering feat, the church structure was built atop the very peak of the mount.*

High above the Normandy flatlands of France, atop the towering rock of Mont-Saint-Michel, stands a unique church complex which represents for many the sum and substance of the Middle Ages. The church originated, according to an old manuscript, as a small chapel constructed in the Eighth Century. The chapel has long since vanished, but today's multilevel structure, built over six centuries, runs the gamut of medieval architecture, from severe early Romanesque to flamboyant late Gothic.

To this famous shrine came pilgrims from every land; kings, priests and peasants worshiped together in the church, and affairs of state were held in the great hall *(opposite)*. A later pilgrim, the American Henry Adams, found here a world in perfect harmony: "Church and State, Soul and Body, God and Man, all are one at Mont-Saint-Michel."

THE GUESTS' HALL, *austere and graceful, was the scene of lavish state functions in the 13th Century, when tables accommodated 200 diners.*

A WORLD PRESERVED, *the medieval church of Mont-Saint-Michel towers high above the encircling town. In 1,000 years, the Mount suffered fire,*

collapsing masonry and wartime attacks. The church survived; its massive spire-crowned bulk shows the power and aspiration of its builders' faith.

GREAT AGES
OF WESTERN
CIVILIZATION

The chart at right is designed to show the duration of the Age of Faith, which forms the subject matter of this volume, and to relate it to the other cultures of the Western world that are considered in one major group of volumes of this series. This chart is excerpted from a comprehensive world chronology which appears in the introductory booklet to the series. Comparison of the chart seen here with the world chronology will enable the reader to relate the great ages of Western civilization to important cultures in other parts of the world.

On the following four pages is printed a chronological table of the important events which took place throughout Western Europe in the epoch covered by this book.

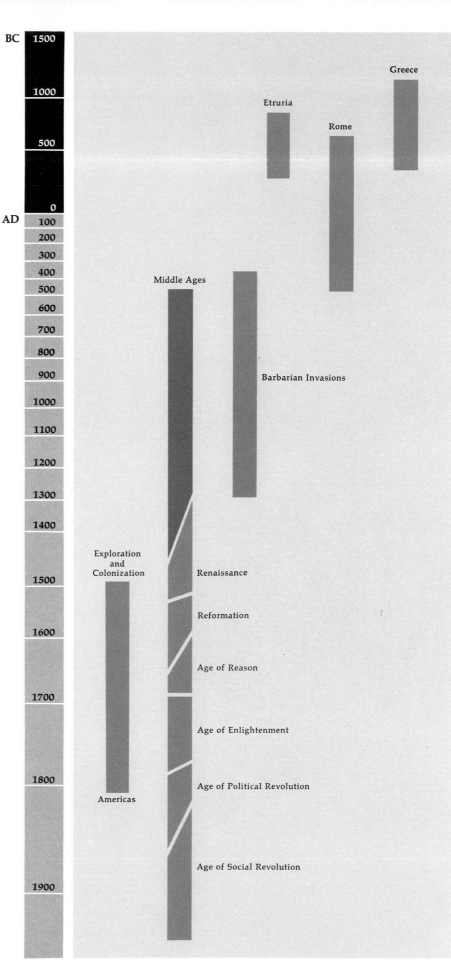

BC 1500
1000
500
0
AD 100
200
300
400
500
600
700
800
900
1000
1100
1200
1300
1400
1500
1600
1700
1800
1900

Greece

Etruria

Rome

Middle Ages

Barbarian Invasions

Exploration and Colonization

Renaissance

Reformation

Age of Reason

Age of Enlightenment

Age of Political Revolution

Americas

Age of Social Revolution

CHRONOLOGY: *A listing of events significant in the Age of Faith*

Church and Papacy	Society and Economics
400	
	Roman tenant-farming system shows tendency towards serfdom
494 Gelasius I, defining spheres of church and state power, declares supremacy of sacred authority	
500	
	European economy increasingly agrarian
c. 529 St. Benedict establishes monastery at Monte Cassino; composes RULE	
563 Irish missionary St. Columba sets out to Iona to convert Picts	**552** Silkworms brought to Constantinople
	585 Famine throughout Gaul
590-604 Gregory I, first monk to become Pope, initiates policies for bringing religious orders under direct papal control	
597 St. Augustine, sent from Rome by Gregory I, begins the conversion of Kent	
600	
622-623 Isidore of Seville writes ETYMOLOGIAE, declaring that sovereign should provide for welfare of Church	*Fusion of Roman and Germanic civilizations and peoples throughout Europe*
Popes defend Italo-Romans against Lombards and delay fall of Byzantine power in Italy	**660** Organ used in church services
700	
716 St. Boniface, "Apostle of Germany," leaves England on first mission to Frisia	*Western European economic development restricted by Moslem control of Mediterranean trade from Seventh to 11th Centuries*
725 Emperor Leo III forbids veneration of sacred images; begins iconoclastic controversy with popes	
Notable confiscation of Church property and appropriation of Church revenue begin in Merovingian Gaul	*Manorial system takes shape in Gaul and Italy*
754 Stephen II receives, from Carolingian King Pepin I, Italian territory and promise of defense against Lombards	
c.779-821 St. Benedict of Aniane leads reform of Benedictine monasteries in France	
800	
	c. 800 Charlemagne's CAPITULARE DE VILLIS on managing a royal manor
	Numerous schools established throughout Charlemagne's Empire
843 Council of Constantinople ends iconoclasm; restores image veneration	
900	
910 Founding of Abbey of Cluny	**c. 900** Salerno a prominent medical center
963 Emperor Otto I, in controversy with papacy, institutes pope's oath of fidelity to emperor before consecration	*Feudalism and manorialism, aided by Carolingian Empire's disintegration, become firmly established*
1000	
c. 1000 Scandinavia and Hungary converted to Christianity	
1054 Greek Church separation begins	
1059 Nicholas II decrees pope henceforth to be elected by cardinals	
1075 Investiture controversy begins between papacy and Empire	
1098 St. Robert of Molesme founds Cistercian Order at Cîteaux	**c. 1090** Guild of weavers at Mainz

Politics

476 Emperor Romulus Augustulus deposed; Odoacer, a Teuton, rules Italy
481 Clovis becomes King of Salian Franks
496 Clovis baptized

507 Clovis conquers Aquitaine, forcing Visigoths back into Spain
511 Clovis dies; Frankish realm divided among his sons
Frankish expansion continues but partitions and civil wars weaken Merovingian kings, strengthen landed nobles
535-553 Emperor Justinian conquers Ostrogoths in Italy

568 Lombards under Alboin invade Italy

592-593 Pope Gregory I, achieving truce with Lombards, wields temporal power

639 Death of Dagobert, last effective Merovingian king
"Major Domus," originally the chief palace official, gradually becomes virtual ruler of Frankish realm

711 Moslems break Visigothic power in Spain

732 Martel, MAJOR DOMUS, defeats Moslems at Poitiers
751 Pepin I elected and anointed King of the Franks, establishing Carolingian line
751 Fall of Ravenna to Lombards marks downfall of Byzantine power in Italy
774 Charlemagne defeats Lombards

800 Pope Leo III crowns Charlemagne Emperor of the West at Rome
814 Louis the Pious succeeds Charlemagne as Emperor

843 Treaty of Verdun partitions Charlemagne's Empire
Viking invasions at height
871-899 Alfred the Great is King of Wessex
887 Final disruption of Carolingian Empire

911 Founding of duchy of Normandy by Norse leader Rollo
962 King Otto I of Germany crowned Emperor of the West, beginning the Holy Roman Empire
987 Hugh Capet elected King of France and establishes Capetian dynasty

1017-1035 Canute the Great of Denmark is King of England

1059-1259 England and France involved in intermittent warfare
1061-1091 Normans conquer Sicily
1066 William of Normandy wins Battle of Hastings

1095-1099 First Crusade establishes Kingdom of Jerusalem

Philosophy, Art and Literature

c. 400 St. Jerome completes Vulgate, standard Latin translation of Bible

523 Boethius writes CONSOLATION OF PHILOSOPHY
532-537 Hagia Sophia built at Constantinople
540 Cassiodorus founds monastic library at Vivarium
Establishment of Exarchate of Ravenna brings Byzantine art to Italy
c. 576 St. Gregory of Tours begins HISTORIA FRANCORUM

c. 593 Pope Gregory I writes DIALOGUES, also contributes to development of plainsong

c. 670 Caedmon of Whitby, versifier of Scripture and earliest-known English lyricist

c. 725 BEOWULF, Anglo-Saxon epic poem, written
731 Venerable Bede completes ECCLESIASTICAL HISTORY OF THE ENGLISH NATION

c. 781 Alcuin invited to establish school at Charlemagne's court
793-804 Cathedral built at Aachen

Preservation of classical literature undertaken during Carolingian Renaissance
840 Einhard, biographer of Charlemagne, dies

999-1003 Taking the name Sylvester II, the great teacher Gerbert reigns as first French Pope

c. 1025 Guido of Arezzo writes MICROLOGUS, theoretical work that strongly influences medieval music
Romanesque period at height

1079-1142 Peter Abelard, French philosopher and teacher, in his lifetime writes SIC ET NON, HISTORIA CALAMITATUM, letters to Heloise, hymns
1086-1126 William IX, Duke of Aquitaine, is first known troubadour

400

500

600

700

800

900

1000

Church and Papacy	Society and Economics
1100	
1107 Investiture controversy settled in England	**c. 1100** Revival in study of Roman law at Bologna
c. 1120 Founding of military orders of Templars and Hospitallers	
1122 Concordat of Worms settles investiture struggle in Germany	*Economic revival: growth of towns and communal governments; increasing population; development of money economy; clearance of waste lands; extensive sheep-raising and growth of wool markets in England and Flanders*
1146 St. Bernard of Clairvaux preaches Second Crusade	**c. 1150** Importation of silk culture to Sicily
	Crusades hasten growth of money economy
1170 Thomas à Becket, Archbishop of Canterbury, murdered by knights of King Henry II	
Spread of Albigensian and Waldensian heresies	**c. 1190** First windmills in Europe
1198-1216 Pontificate of Innocent III marks height of medieval papacy	
1200	
1207-1208 Order of St. Francis formed	**1209** Founding of Cambridge University
1215 Fourth Lateran Council establishes rules for clergy	
1216 Honorius III approves St. Dominic's Order of Friars Preachers	
1233 Gregory IX begins Inquisition for trial of Albigensian heretics in southern France	
1234 Gregory IX issues papal decretals codifying canon law	
1250 Robert Grosseteste, Bishop of Lincoln, protests papal appointments of Italians to English posts	
	1264 Founding of Merton College begins collegiate system at Oxford
	c. 1265 Marco Polo travels to Far East
	c. 1270 Oldest paper manufacturing in Christian Europe at Fabriano
1274-1281 Brief reunion of Roman and Greek Churches	
	c. 1285 Eyeglasses made in northern Italy
	1291 Genoese vessels attempt to circumnavigate Africa
1300	
1302 Boniface VIII's bull UNAM SANCTAM asserts papal supremacy in temporal affairs	
1305 Clement V becomes Pope; moves papacy to Avignon	**c. 1310** Perfection of mechanical clock
1307-1312 Trial and abolishment of Knights Templars	**c. 1320** Use of firearms (small cannon)
c. 1324 Marsiglio of Padua in DEFENSOR PACIS supports conciliarism, the idea that general council, rather than pope, is principal authority of Church	
	1347-1354 Cola di Rienzi, dreaming of Rome's past greatness, leads revolt against nobility
1353-1363 Cardinal Albornoz restores pope's power over Papal States	**1348-1350** Bubonic plague, "The Black Death," at peak
	1358 Revolt of peasants, the Jacquerie, in northern France
1377 Avignon Captivity ends	**1370** Height of Hanseatic League's power
1378 Great Schism in papacy begins; two elected Popes contend for power	
	1381 Peasants' Revolt in England
	1388 First urban sanitary act passed by English Parliament
1400	
1409 Council of Pisa ends with threefold schism	*Social and economic conflict in towns; shift in trade routes and expansion of maritime trade; decline of overland trade with Far East and search for new routes*
1414-1418 Council of Constance ends Great Schism	
1431 St. Joan of Arc burned at Rouen	
1438 Charles VII of France issues PRAGMATIC SANCTION OF BOURGES, establishing liberty of Gallican Church	**c. 1450** Invention of printing with movable type

Politics	Philosophy, Art and Literature	
1100 Henry I of England forced to sign Charter of Liberties	**c.1100** CHANSON DE ROLAND written	**1100**
1135-1154 Turbulent civil war in England	**c.1136** Geoffrey of Monmouth writes HISTORY OF THE KINGS OF BRITAIN	
	c.1142 Peter Lombard writes SENTENCES, a standard textbook of theology during the Middle Ages	
1147-1149 Second Crusade fails to recapture Edessa from Turks		
1164 Constitutions of Clarendon extend jurisdiction of English civil courts at expense of church courts	**1163** Cathedral of Notre Dame, Paris, begun	
	Beginning of Gothic style in art and architecture	
1167 Venice forms Lombard League of northern Italian cities	*Development of vernacular literature*	
	c.1170 Chrétien de Troyes is first great poet of Arthurian cycle	
1189-1192 Third Crusade fails to recapture Jerusalem		
	c.1200 POEMA DEL CID written in Castile	**1200**
1202-1204 Fourth Crusade establishes Latin Empire	**c.1203** NIBELUNGENLIED written in southern Germany	
1208-1229 Albigensian Crusades, by ruining nobles of southern France, strengthen power of kings		
1215 King John signs Magna Carta		
1217-1221 Fifth Crusade, to Egypt, fails to destroy Moslem center of strength		
1228-1229 Sixth Crusade recovers Jerusalem, Nazareth and Bethlehem by treaty	*Gothic architecture at zenith*	
	c.1235 LE ROMAN DE LA ROSE begun by Guillaume de Lorris	
1248-1254 Louis IX leads Seventh Crusade to Egypt	*Growth of vernacular literature: French fabliaux, Italian lyric poetry, German minnesang*	
1254-1273 Interregnum in Germany: absence of recognition of any one king's authority	**1260** Cathedral at Chartres consecrated	
1265 Simon de Montfort calls Parliament of lay and spiritual lords, knights, burgesses	**c.1266** Roger Bacon writes OPUS MAIUS	
	1267-1273 St. Thomas Aquinas writes SUMMA THEOLOGICA	
1270 Louis IX dies in Tunis on Eighth Crusade		
1273 Rudolph of Hapsburg elected Emperor	**c.1277** Jean de Meun completes LE ROMAN DE LA ROSE	
1282 Sicilians revolt against Charles of Anjou; Peter of Aragon becomes their King	*Medieval culture reflects secularization of themes and increasing independence from Church influence*	
1291 Forest Cantons form Swiss Confederation		
1302 Philip IV convenes first Estates-General in France at which all three estates are represented		**1300**
	1305-1306 Giotto paints THE LAMENTATION at Padua	
	c.1321 Dante completes DIVINA COMMEDIA	
1337 Outbreak of Hundred Years' War between England and France		
1338 German Diet declares independence of papal approval in election of emperor	**1342** Petrarch writes epic poem AFRICA	
	1348-1353 Boccaccio writes DECAMERONE	
1356-1358 Constitutional crisis in France; Estates-General, led by Parisian merchant Etienne Marcel, attempts reforms		
	c.1375 VISION OF PIERS THE PLOWMAN written by William Langland	
	c.1380 First translation of Bible into English, by followers of John Wycliffe, in progress	
1386 Swiss Confederation defeats the Austrians at Sempach	**c.1387** Chaucer begins CANTERBURY TALES	
		1400
Germany troubled by nobles against crown, bourgeoisie against nobles, rising nationalism	**1420** Brunelleschi begins to build dome for cathedral at Florence	
	1432 Jan van Eyck completes altarpiece in Ghent, major work of early Flemish painting	
1453 Cessation of Hundred Years' War Fall of Constantinople		

BIBLIOGRAPHY

These books were selected during the preparation of the volume for their interest and authority, and for their usefulness to readers seeking additional information on specific points. An asterisk (*) marks works available in both hard-cover and paperback editions; a dagger (†) indicates availability only in paperback.

GENERAL HISTORY

Artz, Frederick B., *The Mind of the Middle Ages A.D. 200-1500*. Alfred A. Knopf, 1958.
*Bloch, Marc, *Feudal Society*. Transl. by L. A. Manyon. University of Chicago Press, 1961.
Cantor, Norman F., *Medieval History*. Macmillan, 1963.
*Coulton, G. G., *Medieval Panorama*. Meridian Books, 1955.
*Coulton, G. G., *Medieval Village, Manor and Monastery*. Peter Smith, 1962.
Durant, Will, *The Story of Civilization. The Age of Faith*. Vol. 4. Simon and Schuster, 1950.
Ferguson, Wallace K., *Europe in Transition, 1300-1520*. Houghton Mifflin, 1962.
†Ganshof, François L., *Feudalism*. Transl. by Philip Grierson. Harper, 1961.
*Haskins, Charles Homer, *The Renaissance of the Twelfth Century*. Peter Smith, 1962.
*Heer, Friedrich, *The Medieval World. Europe 1100-1350*. Transl. by Janet Sondheimer. World Publishing, 1962.
Kelly, Amy, *Eleanor of Aquitaine and the Four Kings*. Harvard University Press, 1950.
The Legacy of the Middle Ages. Ed. by C. G. Crump and E. F. Jacob. Oxford University Press, 1948.
McKisack, May, *The Fourteenth Century, 1307-1399*. Oxford University Press, 1959.
O'Sullivan, Jeremiah, and John F. Burns, *Medieval Europe*. Appleton-Century-Crofts, 1943.
*Painter, Sidney, *French Chivalry: Chivalric Ideas and Practices in Medieval France*. Johns Hopkins, 1940.
†Pirenne, Henri, *Economic and Social History of Medieval Europe*. Transl. by I. E. Clegg. Harcourt, 1956.
*Pirenne, Henri, *Medieval Cities. Their Origins and the Revival of Trade*. Peter Smith, 1962.
*Southern, R. W., *The Making of the Middle Ages*. Yale University Press, 1963.
†Stephenson, Carl, *Medieval Feudalism*. Cornell University Press, 1956.
Strayer, Joseph R., and Dana Carleton Munro, *The Middle Ages, 395-1500*. Appleton-Century-Crofts, 1959.
†Strayer, Joseph R., *Western Europe in the Middle Ages: A Short History*. Appleton-Century-Crofts, 1955.
Thompson, James Westfall, and Edgar Nathaniel Johnson, *An Introduction to Medieval Europe, 300-1500*. W. W. Norton, 1937.
Thompson, James Westfall, *Economic and Social History of the Middle Ages* (2 vols.). Frederick Ungar, 1959.

LEARNING AND LITERATURE

*Curtius, Ernst Robert, *European Literature and the Latin Middle Ages*. Transl. by Willard R. Trask. Pantheon Books, 1953.
†Haskins, Charles Homer, *The Rise of Universities*. Cornell University Press, 1963.
*Huizinga, J., *The Waning of the Middle Ages*. St. Martin's Press, 1949.
Jackson, W.T.H., *The Literature of the Middle Ages*. Columbia University Press, 1960.
*Lewis, C. S., *The Allegory of Love: A Study in Medieval Tradition*. Oxford University Press, 1936.
The Portable Medieval Reader. Ed. by Ross, James Bruce and Mary Martin McLaughlin. The Viking Press, 1960.
Rashdall, Hastings, *The Universities of Europe in the Middle Ages* (3 vols.). Ed. by F. M. Powicke and A. B. Emden. Oxford University Press, 1951.
†Schachner, Nathan. *The Medieval Universities*. A. S. Barnes. 1962.

Thorndike, L., *History of Magic and Experimental Science*. Vols. 1-4. Columbia University Press, 1923-1956.
*Waddell, Helen, *The Wandering Scholars*. Barnes & Noble, 1959.

RELIGION AND PHILOSOPHY

*Dawson, Christopher, *Religion and the Rise of Western Culture*. Sheed & Ward, 1950.
Delatte, Paul, *A Commentary on the Rule of St. Benedict*. Archabbey Press, 1950.
Gontard, Friedrich, *The Chair of Peter. A History of the Papacy*. Transl. by A. J. and E. F. Peeler. Holt, Rinehart and Winston, 1964.
Taylor, Henry Osborn, *The Medieval Mind: A History of the Development of Thought and Emotion in the Middle Ages* (2 vols.) (4th ed.). Harvard University Press, 1959.

DAILY LIFE

*Bennett, H. S., *Life on the English Manor: A Study of Peasant Conditions, 1150-1400*. Cambridge University Press, 1960.
Boissonnade, P. *Life and Work in Medieval Europe*. Transl. by Eileen Power. Alfred A. Knopf, 1927.
Collis, Louise, *Memoirs of a Medieval Woman: The Life and Times of Margery Kempe*. Thomas Y. Crowell, 1964.
Evans, Joan. *Life in Medieval France*. Phaidon Press, London, 1957.
Homans, George Caspar, *English Villagers in the Thirteenth Century*. Russell & Russell, 1960.
*Power, Eileen, *Medieval People*. Barnes & Noble, 1963.

ART AND ARCHITECTURE

*Adams, Henry, *Mont-Saint-Michel and Chartres*. Houghton Mifflin, 1963.
Anthony, Edgar W., *Romanesque Frescoes*. Princeton University Press, 1951.
Conant, Kenneth J., *Carolingian and Romanesque Architecture: 800-1200*. Penguin, 1957.
Evans, Joan, *Art in Medieval France; 987-1498*. Oxford University Press, 1948.
Focillon, Henri, *The Art of the West in the Middle Ages. Volume One, Romanesque Art. Volume Two, Gothic Art*. Transl. by Donald King. Phaidon, 1963.
*Gimpel, Jean, *The Cathedral Builders*. Transl. by Carl Barnes Jr. Peter Smith, 1962.
Larousse Encyclopedia of Byzantine and Medieval Art. Ed. by René Huyghe. Transl. by Dennis Gilbert, Ilse Schreier and Wendela Schurmann. Prometheus Press, 1963.
*Mâle, Emile, *The Gothic Image. Religious Art in France in the Thirteenth Century*. Transl. by Dora Nussey. Peter Smith, 1958.
Morey, Charles Rufus, *Medieval Art*. W. W. Norton, 1942.
Nordenfalk, Carl, and Andre Grabar, *Early Medieval Painting*. Transl. by Stuart Gilbert. World Publishing (Skira series), 1957.
Nordenfalk, Carl, and Andre Grabar, *Romanesque Painting*. World Publishing (Skira series), 1960.
Porcher, Jean, *Medieval French Miniatures*. Harry N. Abrams, 1959.
Rickert, Margaret, *Painting in Britain: The Middle Ages*. Penguin, 1954.
Romanesque Europe. Ed. by Harald Busch and Bernd Lohse, Macmillan, 1960.
*Simson, Otto von, *The Gothic Cathedral*. Pantheon, 1962.

ACKNOWLEDGMENT OF QUOTATIONS

Page 26—From *The Silver Branch* by Sean O'Faolain, Copyright 1938 by The Viking Press, Inc. Reprinted by permission of The Viking Press, Inc. Page 99—From *The Rise of Universities* by Charles Homer Haskins, Cornell University Press, 1963, transl. by J. A. Symonds.

ACKNOWLEDGMENTS

The editors of this book are particularly indebted to Jeremiah F. O'Sullivan, Professor of Medieval History, Fordham University; Harry Bober, Professor of Fine Arts, New York University; John Plummer, Curator of Medieval and Renaissance Manuscripts, Mary Kenway and John Baglow, The Pierpont Morgan Library, New York; Randolph Bullock, Curator of Arms and Armor, and Helmut Nickel, Associate Curator, The Metropolitan Museum of Art, New York; Dorothy Miner, The Walters Art Gallery, Baltimore; Raymond V. Schoder, S. J.; John Paolucci, Prior, Our Lady of Fatima Monastery, Moorestown, New Jersey; Bibliothèque Nationale, Paris; Jean Villette; Department of Manuscripts, British Museum, London; The Staff of the London Museum; Nivardo Buttarazzi, Abbot, Abbazia di Casamari; Bruno Papera, Director, Biblioteca Governativa, Lucca; Olga Marinelli, Director, Biblioteca Augusta, Perugia; Father Guy Ferrari, Vatican Library, Rome; General Arnaldo Forgero, Director, and Colonel Eugenio Panasci, Castel Sant' Angelo, Rome; Emanuele Casamassima, Biblioteca Nazionale, Rome; Idlefonso Tassi, Librarian, San Paolo Fuori Le Mura, Rome; Mario Pinzuti, Director, Istituto Restauro Scientifico del Libro, Rome; Gustav Hofmann, Director, Bayerische Staatsbibliothek, Munich; Erich Steingräber, Director, Germanisches Nationalmuseum, Nuremberg; Carl Wehmer, Heidelberg Universitätsbibliothek; Bildarchiv Foto Marburg; Historisches Bildarchiv, Bad Berneck; Historia Foto, Bad Sachsa; Ann Munchow, Aachen; Natalia Hochstein, Munich; Bruno Thomas, Director, and Ortwin Gamber, Kunsthistorisches Museum, Vienna; Walter Hummelberger, Historisches Museum der Stadt Wien.

ART INFORMATION AND PICTURE CREDITS

The sources for the illustrations in this book are set forth below. Credits for pictures positioned from left to right are separated by semicolons, from top to bottom by dashes.

Photographers' names which follow a descriptive note appear in parentheses. Abbreviations include "MS." for manuscript, "ca." for circa and "c." for century.

Cover—"La Belle Verrière," stained-glass window, Chartres Cathedral, 12th c. (Gjon Mili).

CHAPTER 1: 10—"Christ in Majesty," illumination from *Evangélaire de Charlemagne* by the scribe Godescalc, ca. 781, MS. Nouv. acq. Lat. 1203, folio 3, Bibliothèque Nationale, Paris, Publications Filmées d'Art et d'Histoire. 13—Jelling Stone from Denmark, 10th c., National Museum, Copenhagen. 14-15—Drawing by Victor and Maria Lazzaro. 17—Bronze seal of Raimon de Mondragon, from Provence, 12th c., Cabinet de Médailles, Bibliothèque Nationale, Paris (Ina Brady)—bronze tithe vessel, 13th c., Cluny Museum, Paris (E. Van der Veen). 18—Bronze statuette of Charlemagne, 9th c., Louvre Museum, Paris (Giraudon). 21-29—Illuminations from *Hours of the Virgin*, from Flanders, ca. 1515, MS. 399, The Pierpont Morgan Library, New York (Hans R. Lippmann).

CHAPTER 2: 30—*Essen Madonna*, reliquary statue, gold over wooden core, 10th c., Essen Cathedral, Germany (Gjon Mili). 33—Drawing by Victor and Maria Lazzaro after 9th c. plan, Chapter Library, St. Gall Monastery, Switzerland. 35—Carved ivory panel, from western Germany or Lorraine, 10th c., Kunsthistorisches Museum, Vienna. 37—Pyx, gilded copper and enamel, from Limoges, 13th c., National Gallery of Art, Washington, D.C.—crosier, gilded copper and enamel, 13th c., Treasury of the Cathedral of Lyon (Luc Joubert). 41-51—Photographs by David Lees.

CHAPTER 3: 52—Stone tomb sculpture, from northeastern France, ca. 1163, Chapel of the Greyfriars Monastery, Nancy (Robert Mottar). 55—Parchment letter from bishops of the Holy Land to King Philip Augustus of France, 1220, Musée de l'Histoire de France, Paris, from *Dans les Pas des Croisés*, Librairie Hachette, Paris (Cliché Frederique Duran). 57—Pilgrim badge of St. Thomas of Canterbury, pewter, 14th-15th c., courtesy of the Trustees of the London Museum (Heinz Zinram). 58—Ife Yoruba Memorial Figure, bronze, probably 13th c., Ife Museum, Nigeria (Eliot Elisofon). 61—Illumination from *Liber divinorum operum*, visions of St. Hildegard of Bingen, from Germany early 13th c., MS. 1942, folio 27 verso, Biblioteca Governativa, Lucca (Emmett Bright). 62-63—Illumination from *Le Songe du Pèlerinage* by Guillaume de Digulleville, from Flanders, ca. 1380-1390, MS. 10176-8, folio 68, Bibliothèque Royale, Brussels—stone sculpture by Gislebertus, from Cathedral of St. Lazarus, Autun, 12th c., Rolin Museum, Autun (Dmitri Kessel). 64—Sculptured stone capital by Gislebertus, Cathedral of St. Lazarus, Autun, 12th c. (Dmitri Kessel). 65—Illumination from *Speculum Virginum* by Vincent de Beauvais, from Swabia, 12th c., MS. Arundel 44, folio 93 verso, British Museum, London. 66—Sculptured stone reliefs by Gislebertus, Cathedral of St. Lazarus, Autun, 12th c. (Dmitri Kessel). 67—Illumination from the *Psalter of Henry of Blois* (Bishop of Winchester), 12th c., MS. Cotton Nero C. IV, folio 39, British Museum, London. 68—Sculptured stone relief by Gislebertus, Cathedral of St. Lazarus, Autun, 12th c. (Dmitri Kessel). 69—Illumination from *Apocalypse of Saint-Sever*, from Gascony, 11th c., MS. Latin 8878, folio 121 recto, Bibliothèque Nationale, Paris.

CHAPTER 4: 70—Detail from *Good Government* by Ambrogio Lorenzetti, fresco, 14th c., Palazzo Pubblico, Siena (David Lees). 72—David Greenspan, courtesy of C. S. Hammond & Co. 76-77—Drawing from *Liber de Assisa Panis*, 1293, Guildhall Record Office, London, courtesy of the Corporation of London. 79—Illumination from *Le Livre du Gouvernement des Princes* by Gilles Romain, from 16th c. translation of 15th c. original, MS. Rés. 5062, folio 149 verso, Bibliothèque de l'Arsenal, Paris (Bulloz). 80-81—Lapie-Photothèque Française. 82-83—Illumination from *Pontifical de Sens*, 14th c., MS. Latin 962, folio 264, Bibliothèque Nationale, Paris; illumination attributed to the Monk of Hyeres, from Genoa, 14th c., MS. Additional 27695, folio 7 verso, British Museum, London—illumination from *Caesar's Commentaries*, Book IV, 15th c., MS. Douce 208, folio 120 verso, Bodleian Library, Oxford. 84—Illumination from *Des Proprietez des Choses*, by Jean du Ries, from Bruges, 1482, MS. Royal 15 E. II, folio 265, British Museum, London. 85—Illumination from Sir John Mandeville's *Book of Travels*, from Liège, 15th c., MS. Additional 24189, folio 16, British Museum, London—illumination from *Des Proprietez des Choses*, by Jean du Ries, from Bruges, 1482, MS. Royal 15 E. III, folio 269, British Museum, London. 86—Illumination attributed to the Monk of Hyeres, from Genoa, 14th c., MS. Additional 27695, folio 14, British Museum, London. 87—Illumination from *Biblical History*, by Guyart des Moulins, executed by Jean du Ries, from Bruges, 1470, MS. Royal 15 D. I, folio 18, British Museum, London. 88-89—Street in Sermonetta, Italy (Emmett Bright); illumination from *Miroir Historial* by Vincent de Beauvais, 14th c., MS. Rés. 5080, folio 373, Bibliothèque de l'Arsenal, Paris—illumination from "La Peste à Tournay" from the *Annals* by Gilles le Muisit, 14th c., MS. 13077, folio 24 recto, Bibliothèque Royale, Brussels. 90-91—Illumination from book of statutes of the Perugia notaries college, 14th c., MS. 972, folio 2 verso, Biblioteca Augusta, Perugia (Emmett Bright); illumination from Froissart's *Chronicles*, from France, 15th c., MS. Harley 4379, folio 64, British Museum, London.

CHAPTER 5: 92—*The Lady and the Unicorn*, tapestry representing the sense of touch, 1500-1510, Cluny Museum, Paris (Robert Mottar). 95—Seal of the University of Paris, silver in iron setting, 13th c., Cabinet des Médailles, Bibliothèque Nationale, Paris. 97—Illumination from *Manafi al-Hayawan*, by Ibn Bakhtishu, 13th c., MS. 500, folio 37, The Pierpont Morgan Library, New York. 98—Drawing by Matthew Paris from *Liber Experimentarius* by Bernardus Silvestris, 13th c., MS. Ashmole 304, folio 31 verso, The Bodleian Library, Oxford. 100-101—Illumination from "The Arnstein Bible," from the Premonstratensian Abbey, Arnstein, ca. 1175, MS. Harley 2799, folio 243, British Museum, London. 103—Illumination from the *Luttrell Psalter*, c. 1340, MS. Additional 42130, folio 202 verso, British Museum, London. 104-105—Illumination from *Chansonnier de Montpellier*, 13th-14th c., MS. H. 196, Bibliothèque de la Faculté de Médecine, Montpellier (Robert Lackenbach from Black Star); illumination from *Manesse Liederhandschrift*, 14th c., MS. 848, folio 149, Heidelberg University Library (Robert Lackenbach from Black Star); illumination from *Le Roman de Troie*, by Benoit de Sainte-Maure, 14th c., MS. Français 782, folio 161, Bibliothèque Nationale, Paris—illumination from untitled manuscript, 14th c., MS. Français 1136, folio 86, Bibliothèque Nationale, Paris. 106-107—Illumination from *Chroniques de France*, 14th c., MS. Royal 16 G. VI, folio 442, British Museum, London—illumination from *Les Estoires d'Outremer*, by William of Tyre, 13th c., MS. Français 2630, folio 22 verso, Bibliothèque Nationale, Paris; illumination from the *Life and Miracles of St. Louis* by Guillaume de Saint-Pathus, 14th c., MS. Français 5716, page 40, Bibliothèque Nationale, Paris. 108-109—Carved ivory casket, from France, 14th c., National Museum, Ravenna (Emmett Bright). 110—Illumination from *Histoire d'Olivier de Castille*, from Flanders, 15th c., MS. Français 12.574, folio 181 verso, Bibliothèque Nationale, Paris—illumination from *Book of Chess of Alfonso the Wise*, 13th c., MS. j. T. 6, folio 9 recto, Library of El Escorial monastery, Spain, photograph granted through the courtesy of the Patrimonio Nacional (Robert Mottar). 111—Illumination from *Très Riches Heures* of the Duc de Berry, ca. 1416, MS. 65 (1284), August, Musée Condé, Chantilly (Giraudon). 112-113—Illumination from *Roman de la Rose*, from Flanders, 15th c., MS. Harley 4425, folio 12 verso, British Museum, London (Frank Scherschel); ivory mirror-back, 14th c., Cluny Museum, Paris, Cultural History Research, Inc. 114-115—Illumination from *La Quête du Saint Graal et la Morte d'Arthur*, from Italy, 14th c., MS. Français 343, folio 7, Bibliothèque Nationale, Paris.

CHAPTER 6: 116—Illumination from a commentary by St. Augustin on the psalms, 13th c., MS. 19, folio 2, Bibliothèque Municipale de Douai (Giraudon). 118—Drawing from the *Album* by Villard de Honnecourt, 13th c., MS. Français 19093, folio 36, Bibliothèque Nationale, Paris. 120-121—Drawings by Victor and Maria Lazzaro. 124—Illumination from "Missal" for Paris use, ca. 1380, MS. 10.124, folio 111, The Walters Art Gallery, Baltimore—Music Book Associates. 127-139—Photographs by Gjon Mili.

CHAPTER 7: 140—Detail from the *Wilton Diptych*, painted panel, from France, ca. 1395, courtesy of the Trustees of the National Gallery, London (Derek Bayes). 144-145—Consanguinity table from *Decretum Gratiani*, from Salzburg, 12th c., MS. CLM 13004, Bayerische Staatsbibliothek, Munich. 149—Face of clock, Wells Cathedral, England (Derek Bayes)—mechanism of Wells Cathedral clock, The Science Museum, London. 151—Armor for man and horse, from Italy, 15th c., The Metropolitan Museum of Art, New York, Rogers Fund, 1904 (Jon Naar). 152-153—Top details from the Bayeux Tapestry, 11th c., Bayeux Cathedral, from *The Bayeux Tapestry*, edited by Sir Frank Stenton, published by Phaidon Press, Ltd., London (Percy Hennell)—detail from Bayeux Tapestry (Giraudon). 154-155—Detail from the "Courtrai Chest," wood, from Flanders, 14th c., courtesy the Warden and Fellows of New College, Oxford (Heinz Zinram)—crossbow, 15th c., Kunsthistorisches Museum, Vienna (Erich Lessing from Magnum). 156—Illumination from *Siege of Orléans*, 15th c., MS. Français 5054, folio 54 verso, Bibliothèque Nationale, Paris. 157—15th c., cannon, Castel Sant' Angelo, Rome (Roloff Beny).

CHAPTER 8: 158—*St. Francis* by Cimabue, fresco, c. 1280, Church of St. Francis, Assisi (Marzari). 163—"Danse Macabre," from a printed book, 1486, Rés. Ye. 189, Bibliothèque Nationale, Paris, Cultural History Research, Inc. 165—Sketch of Joan of Arc by Clement de Fauquembergue in the margin of the official story of the siege of Orléans, ink on parchment, 1429, Archives Nationales, Paris, Cultural History Research, Inc. 167-179—Photographs by Gjon Mili.

INDEX

*This symbol in front of a page number indicates a photograph or painting of the subject mentioned.

XXX

PRODUCTION STAFF FOR TIME INCORPORATED

John L. Hallenbeck (Vice President and Director of Production),
Robert E. Foy, Caroline Ferri and Don Sheldon
Text photocomposed under the direction of Albert J. Dunn and Arthur J. Dunn